PROBLEMS IN THE HISTORY AND PHILOSOPHY OF PHYSICAL EDUCATION AND SPORT

Prentice-Hall Foundations of Physical Education Series

JOHN E. NIXON
Stanford University
Series Editor

PROBLEMS IN THE HISTORY AND PHILOSOPHY OF PHYSICAL EDUCATION AND SPORT

Earle F. Zeigler
Ph.D.
University of Illinois

PRENTICE-HALL, INC., ENGLEWOOD CLIFFS, NEW JERSEY

194587

GV
342
Z43

PRENTICE-HALL INTERNATIONAL, INC., London
PRENTICE-HALL OF AUSTRALIA, PTY. LTD., Sydney
PRENTICE-HALL OF CANADA, LTD., Toronto
PRENTICE-HALL OF INDIA PRIVATE LTD., New Delhi
PRENTICE-HALL OF JAPAN, INC., Tokyo

Series Preface

The purpose of the *Foundations of Physical Education* series is to provide a set of textbooks which, by presenting selected generalizations from related fields of knowledge, contribute to a sophisticated understanding of physical education as an academic discipline. These validated generalizations provide a sound basis for educational decision-making by teachers, coaches, supervisors, and administrators at all school levels.

Physical education currently is defined as the art and science of voluntary, purposeful human movement. Its central concern is man engaging in selected motor performances and the meaning and significance of these experiences. Thus, physical education is a broad cross-disciplinary subject. It requires of its scholars and practitioners a command of the most relevant generalizations, being generated in the closely related disciplines, which describe and explain phenomena associated with human movement. Those disciplines which provide the most relevant foundational knowledge for physical education are physiology, neurology, psychology, sociology, anthropology, history, philosophy, anatomy, and kinesiology.

Present physical education texts generally fail to treat in depth relevant generalizations from related disciplines. In these books, one or two physical education authors have attempted to present a series of "principles" of physical education in a few chapters, each of which contains some reference to knowledge in various fields. In today's world of rapidly expanding knowledge, one or two authors can no longer be well versed in several disciplines sufficiently to write principles and foundations books in physical education, which possess the depth and sophistication required to understand and describe the field, and to guide its practices.

With rare exceptions, scholars of other disciplines have not devoted their major attention to investigation and reports which concern physical education phenomena. Thus, for example, the historians have virtually neglected the history of sport in general history books and few sociologists have studied sports as their major line of inquiry.

Nonetheless a vast accumulation of knowledge exists in the literature of the foundation fields which has direct and essential relevance to physical education. Most of this knowledge has not been accumulated systematically or reported and interpreted accurately to the physical education profession. The task of selecting and reporting relevant generalizations from any one discipline requires a physical education scholar who is also a scholar of the related subject.

For the first time in physical education literature, this series incorporates books about physical education, prepared by distinguished physical education scholars, who have established reputations for knowledge and competence in the subject matter and in the principal modes of inquiry in the related fields. Thus, each volume synthesizes recent knowledge into usable form for students and teachers and is unique in physical education literature. Furthermore, the reader is instructed in the process of developing his own *principles* of physical education from his increasing knowledge and understanding. Comprehensive bibliographies list basic references for further study in each field.

This series is appropriate for Foundations or Principles of Physical Education courses at both the undergraduate and graduate levels. Individual volumes are suitable for courses concerning their respective subject areas. Also, these books are valuable for collateral reading and can provide the basis for individual study projects.

The series provides a reference source for the latest knowledge of scientific, behavioral, and humanistic insight and understanding, which constitute the subject and the practice of physical education today. It belongs in the library of every student and teacher of physical education.

J. N.

Preface

There are at present a number of histories of physical education in English and other languages. Also, the titles of many volumes include the words "philosophy" or "principles." The question may well be asked, therefore, if another book is needed with both "history" and "philosophy" in its title. Something new usually appears either because new sources demand that earlier histories be updated or because changing times and resultant new purposes demand that we look at our past differently because of an altered system of values. This volume fulfills both purposes to a degree. It is designed primarily to offer a "persistent or recurring problems approach" to the history and philosophy of physical, health, and recreation education.[1] Following each chapter or section, each problem is analyzed in terms of the leading philosophical tendencies in the Western world.

The author would like to say that the idea for this new approach came to him in a brilliant flash of insight while atop a high mountain, but, alas, the occurrence was much more prosaic. Although many of the specific ideas originated with him and some of his colleagues and graduate students, the credit for this unique approach must go to John S. Brubacher, long-time professor of the history and philosophy of education at Yale and currently a professor of higher education at the University of Michigan. Thus, it is the adaptation of this approach, the selection of certain persistent problems, and the delineation of the implications for this field that may possibly be considered as new contributions. Of course, Professor Brubacher should not be held accountable for possible deficiencies in the transferral.

Some concepts and statements in this book remind us that the second half of this century may come to be known as the time when scholars and research-minded leaders in our field became truly concerned with the need to develop bodies of knowledge from related areas of study. The accumulation

---

[1] No apology is being offered now for calling the field "physical, health, and recreation education." The term could be attributed to a progressive outlook; actually it merely intimates that we are concerned with many aspects of man's total education. If we grant that the human being is a total organism, it follows that there is no such thing as *physical* education. However, a need does exist for "physical education"; our problem is to define the term so that the task can be accomplished most effectively.

of this knowledge may well enable the profession, within a reasonable period, to assume what many of us already believe is our rightful role in education and society at large. As the late Dean Arthur S. Daniels remarked at a unique conference of the Big Ten Physical Education Directors at the University of Illinois in December, 1964:

> If we are to gain greater recognition in the academic world, we must follow pathways similar to those traversed by other disciplines. This means a greatly expanded program of scholarly research and development in which the body of knowledge in physical education is defined as nearly as possible in terms of its fundamental nature, and in its relationships with other disciplines.

History and philosophy are two related disciplines from which we must seek guidance, as well as their corresponding subdivisions—the history and philosophy of education. Our profession must be aware of where it has been, how it developed, what its persistent problems are, and what it should do about them. Sound historical and philosophical research, plus investigation of a descriptive nature related to administration as a developing social science, is the type of endeavor to which our best minds should be devoted in increasing numbers. Scientific research of a more basic nature is most important, but we *cannot* afford to slight these other avenues of research. A greater amount of scientific truth is absolutely essential, but men *act* according to their own systems of ethical and/or religious values.

For these reasons, curriculum planners in professional preparation for physical, health, and recreation education should incorporate an articulated series of course experiences in the areas of professional orientation, history, philosophy, and administration *in that order in every curriculum*. Such course experiences, each offered on the basis of prerequisites, are just as important in the development of a professional physical educator as zoology, human anatomy and physiology, kinesiology and physiology of exercise, therapeutic exercise, and other courses that might be included in this sequence. Coupled with professional courses should be basic arts courses such as history, philosophy, English, and the necessary social and natural sciences and courses in general professional education.

This volume in the Prentice-Hall series on Physical Education is based on the historical and philosophical research of this author and many colleagues within and outside this specialized field. The contents are introductory in nature and should be regarded as such. Other volumes in the series will be based on more scientific generalizations available through the efforts of researchers in physical education and related disciplines. Such an approach was not possible here—hence the introduction of selected persistent problems that are traced historically and analyzed philosophically.

If the professional student is able to obtain an early understanding of the nature of these persistent historical problems and how they should be resolved according to the leading philosophical positions in the Western world (a most provincial term nowadays), this volume may stimulate him to greater depth of thought than he may have engaged in otherwise. One last word—do not automatically accept what this book and your teachers tell you. This field desperately needs intelligent, inquiring, and dedicated researchers, teachers of teachers, and professional practitioners. Our future depends on you.

E. F. Z.

Contents

I

Introduction

The significant advances made in the world in the last quarter century have been assessed by Henry Steele Commager, the noted Amherst historian (*Look,* June 6, 1961). Despite the presence of a great deal of evil, he felt that the forces of good had gone steadfastly ahead. But he expressed some fear, because so many "benign achievements also have their malign sides." The major areas in which he felt progress had been made include: 1) the survival of civilization; 2) the end of Western colonialism; 3) the vast progress in natural sciences; 4) the development of electronics; 5) the formidable advances in medical science; 6) the creation and growth of the United Nations; 7) the acceptance of responsibility for the welfare of less fortunate nations; 8) the rapid growth of Big Government (can it do the job?); 9) the unprecedented educational revolution, especially in America; and 10) the recognition of intellectual and material equality that eventually will destroy artificial inequalities of class, race, or color.

OUR BODY OF KNOWLEDGE

These historical occurrences, social influences, scientific discoveries, and inventions all hold implications for the field of education, and hence for physical, health, and recreation education. They have caused leaders in the field to become concerned about the body of knowledge upon which our developing profession is based.[1] The "knowledge explosion" has caught up

---

[1] Much of this introductory material was taken from a paper presented at the 1964 Meeting of the Western Conference (Big Ten) Directors of Physical Education, Urbana, Illinois, Dec. 10, 1964.

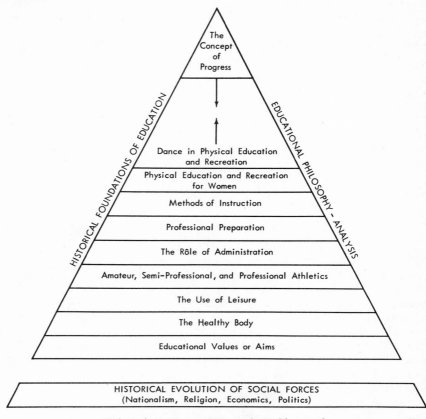

The
Concept
of
Progress

EDUCATIONAL FOUNDATIONS OF EDUCATION

EDUCATIONAL PHILOSOPHY - ANALYSIS

Dance in Physical Education
and Recreation

Physical Education and Recreation
for Women

Methods of Instruction

Professional Preparation

The Rôle of Administration

Amateur, Semi-Professional, and Professional Athletics

The Use of Leisure

The Healthy Body

Educational Values or Aims

HISTORICAL EVOLUTION OF SOCIAL FORCES
(Nationalism, Religion, Economics, Politics)

**Selected Persistent Historical Problems of
Physical, Health, and Recreation Education**

with us, just as it has with our colleagues in other areas of education, and the increase of knowledge in a geometric ratio threatens to engulf us. We are faced with the absolute necessity of "re-tooling" and upgrading our research efforts in universities. In the process we will need to structure our graduate programs in order to prepare highly competent research workers who can understand and assess the knowledge which is available to us from a multitude of disciplines. Many of these disciplines, some of which we are only dimly aware, are our related fields and/or foundation sciences. We will be successful as a profession to the extent that we are able to assimilate this knowledge and the resultant ordered generalizations that have meaning for us. It will then be necessary for researchers in physical, health, and recreation education to set up tentative hypotheses, based on the findings of scholars and scientists in related fields and in our own, and to apply the various methods of research with careful, painstaking investigation to problems which belong uniquely to our profession. This task belongs to us alone. No other discipline will do this for us, except in a secondary way and belatedly. No other generation of physical educators has ever faced such an enormous problem. It is fortunate that we are aware of it, but at present we are poorly prepared to meet it, and time is short.

The potentialities for pure and applied research in physical education and sport are limitless. This is especially true because of the nature of the field and its possible relationships with physiology, anatomy, psychology (and educational psychology), sociology, history, economics, political science, philosophy, anthropology, chemistry, medicine, and theory of administration. At the moment it is not possible to predict accurately where the future may lead research workers in this field. As past research is viewed historically, and as present practices and research investigation are examined through available descriptive research techniques, it is possible only to conjecture about the directions in which the field may hope to move.

At one university (the University of Illinois, for example), it is recognized that the research undertaking in physical education and sport, not to mention efforts in health and safety education as well as recreation and park administration, must both consolidate and expand in order to face future demands and needs adequately. The administrative officers will have to be on the alert for the brightest young minds in the profession. These people will be attracted only if they see evidence of a continuing and broadening program of research, teaching, and service. It is with these thoughts in mind that the following avenues of research were recommended for the Graduate Department of Physical Education:

1. Physical Fitness (Exercise Physiology)
2. Biomechanics (Kinesiology & Movement Analysis)
3. Sport Psychology (Social Aspects and Motor Learning)
4. Historical Investigation (including Oral History)
5. Philosophical Investigation (Normative and Analytical)
6. Theory and Research in Administration
7. Sociological Investigation
8. Comparative Physical Education and Sport
9. Economics and Political Science
10. Anthropology [2]

HISTORY OF PHYSICAL EDUCATION AND SPORT

Having considered the question of research broadly, we may now turn our attention to investigating the history of physical education and sport. The "body of knowledge" is the immediate topic under consideration. Knowledge has been variously defined as "that which is gained and preserved by knowing"; "enlightenment"; "learning"; also, broadly, "the sum of information

---

[2] "Discussion of Present and Future Research Space Needs," a report presented to Dean King J. McCristal, College of Physical Education, University of Illinois, June, 1964, by Professors Cureton, Jackson, Noble, and Zeigler.

conserved by civilization." Wise men appreciate that knowledge accumulation is only part of the task; understanding and wisdom are those attributes for which we really strive. But our attention is focused on knowledge at the moment. Where does our field stand in this matter of historical knowledge today? What do we know? How well do we know it? What don't we know? Can it be discovered? What will we need to know to meet the demands of the future?

Before these questions related to the role that historical research can play in physical education can be answered, it seems desirable to consider briefly the scholarly discipline of history itself. Nevins explains its function as follows (1962, p. 14):

> Although when we use the word history we instinctively think of the past, this is an error, for history is actually a bridge connecting the past with the present, and pointing the road to the future. . . .
>
> This conception of history as a lantern carried by the side of man, moving forward with every step taken, is of course far ampler than the concept of a mere interesting tale to be told, a vivid scene to be described, or a group of picturesque characters to be delineated. It is essentially Western and modern.

Still further, the question might be asked, "What *is* history?" Is everything historic? Are we referring to the actual order of events as seen by an interpreter (the historian)? A student of history might ask whether the philosophy of history challenges the democratic way of life. This would imply, of course, that there is just one way of looking at history or that there is simply one philosophy. If there are a number of philosophies of history, however, what is necessary before we may say that one is paramount?

Approaching the problem from another angle, we might question the validity and reliability of historical research itself. Is it possible to construct a valid philosophy of history that is fact and not fiction? What constitutes acceptable history? Is a simple chronological listing of events satisfactory? Some would argue that history must show the connection between a series of events. It has been said that good history has depth as well as surface, and we can appreciate that it is virtually impossible for the writer of history to eliminate personal feeling and bias.

Returning to Nevins again, long considered one of America's great historians, let us consider his fine, clear definition of the work of the historian (1962, p. 29):

> Not only is the intention of true history high, but the method is scientific. The historian, that is, collects his data fairly, observes it systematically, organizes it logically, and tests its parts thoroughly. Then by inductive logic and the use of hypothesis he reaches provisional generalizations, and only when he has carried out a final search for new data, and made fresh tests, does he commit final conclusions. In all this he casts off, so far as possible, the prejudice of race, nationality, class, and faction. If his method falls short of the test-tube precision of the chemist, it is at any rate as scientific as he can make it. He will go to the primary sources for as many facts as possible, and restrict his reliance on secondary accounts. He will give each

category of evidence its proper valuation: the official document, the letter, the memoir, the newspaper story, the pamphlet, the artifact. He will put every witness, every scrap of paper, under cross-examination. And when he finishes his reconstruction of the past, he will give it as veracious a glow of life as his art can encompass.

These are noble words, and beautifully written. But we must return to reality and ask ourselves once again, "What is the body of historical knowledge in physical, health, and recreation education (including sport)?" To answer this question honestly, the admission must be made that the contribution of physical education historians is, relatively speaking, quite meager indeed, and that the quality of this work typically leaves much to be desired. This comment is not meant to be harsh and critical. All of us who are concerned appreciate the contributions that *have* been made (for example, Van Dalen, Mitchell, and Bennett, *A World History of Physical Education*). Those of us who have contributed in small or larger measure to this "body of knowledge" realize full well the inadequacy of our efforts. Some have done much better than others, and much fine material exists in languages other than English. Our provinciality in this regard makes this material largely unavailable at present.

"As late as 1880 there were only eleven professors of history in American colleges." Muller (1952, pp. 33–34) points out, however, that:

> Our age is nevertheless more historically minded than any previous age, and has a much longer, wider, clearer view of the past. Its contributions to historical knowledge, over the last hundred years, are among its most honorable achievements.

This means that there is hope for physical education yet, if we will but see the need and prepare our own historians of physical education and sport with the readily available help of true historical scholars.

The truth is, however, that we are just beginning to be aware of this need. A few years ago, this writer encouraged a potentially outstanding scholar to concentrate his graduate work on the history and philosophy of physical education, by emphasizing the great need for people like him in our field, and suggesting that he should be able to secure a position in a university where he could carry on his work. However, the young man became so discouraged by the lack of demand for his services that he almost left the field. Fortunately, he has now been employed by a large university and will continue his efforts along the lines of his talent and interest. It must be confessed, though, that he was hired primarily as an administrator and undergraduate counselor, although he will be spending a certain smaller portion of his time in graduate teaching and scholarly investigation. But what has happened to others who down through the years undertook dissertations of an historical or philosophical nature? Why haven't they "produced" in these areas since they completed their degrees? Was their burden in other on-the-job tasks too onerous? Did they lose interest, because there was too little opportunity for cross-fertilization of ideas with their "activity-minded" colleagues in physical education and with other scholars in related disciplines? The answer to both of these questions probably is yes. The climate was not right, and furthermore, the background preparation of these people for this type of endeavor was not sufficiently rigorous.

It is fortunate indeed that history has become so popular, and that significant contributions have been made to historical knowledge. Many primary sources have been uncovered, which can be of great aid to physical education. A certain amount of assistance is available from educational historians as well, but it is true that they have typically shunned physical education and sport for several reasons. Woody deprecates the fact that those who have written about education and its history have slighted "physical culture" perhaps through bias (1949, vii):

> Despite the fact that lip-service has been paid increasingly to the dictum "a sound mind in a sound body," ever since Western Europe began to revive the educational concepts of the Graeco-Roman world, there is still a lack of balance between physical and mental culture, both in school programs and among those who write of education. This is evident in many quarters, even where a certain universality of outlook ought to reign. Turn where one will, it is impossible to find physical culture adequately presented in books dealing with the general history of education. Written in keeping with a dominant rationalism, these books have been concerned chiefly with intellectual movements and institutions for mental improvement.

Furthermore, Brickman takes many of his colleagues in general professional education to task when he criticizes much of their literary output sharply (1949, Pref.). He decries "the perennial tendency toward dogmatism, superficiality, repetitiousness, and bombast." He makes a strong plea for improved scholarship, as he asserts that "the more education makes use of the recognized techniques of scholarly inquiry, the better will be its chance of attaining first-class citizenship in the academic community."

quality of our effort

Lest we be a bit smug about this criticism of our colleagues in general professional education, we should take heed of Professor Brickman's comments about our own efforts in physical education history. About one well-known history text, he says (p. 23), "some of the chapters are superficial, while some are overloaded with material of dubious value." Another early edition of a standard history of physical education is said (p. 27) to be "an extremely elementary treatment of the subject from primitive times to the present. Informative on the American period. The bibliographies are good, but little use of them has been made in the text." His most damning thrust is leveled at another physical education history as follows (p. 28): "A documented, detailed treatment based, to a large extent, upon secondary sources."

He does have a kind word for one history of physical education (p. 32) that ninety-nine per cent of our physical educators have probably never even heard about—"The most scholarly and thoroughgoing history of physical education in ancient times. Rich documentation from primary source materials." But who wrote it? It was written by Thomas Woody, a solid, educational historian.

It is true that a fair amount of sport history has been written, and much of it is of good quality. But, by and large, we cannot take credit for this work. Physical educators have written a number of master's and doctoral theses on historical topics, but the quality of this work is usually not high. Generally speaking, the people who wrote these theses were not first-rate scholars trained in historiography. Nor were their thesis advisers trained historians! We do not mean to be overly critical of these efforts. They represent a start—quite a good start in fact, especially when we consider other historical efforts of this nature in related academic fields. Further historical studies in physical education could be related to the following types of topics: time period, geographical region, educational level, educational institutions, biography, innovations, philosophy, methodology, curriculum, personnel, comparative education, children, legislations, materials, nonschool agencies, professional organizations, finance, architecture, administration, periodicals and other literature, influence of individuals, comparison of theories, legal liability, sport, economics, and politics. A major related problem is that the instructors teaching our history courses at the undergraduate and graduate levels are typically not very knowledgeable about some of the better representative historical writing that has been accomplished *even* in our own field!

At present the seven graduate professors who are concerned with the history of physical education and sport at the University of Illinois, for example, are attempting to discover, list, abstract, and assess every historical investigation related to this aspect of our graduate research and teaching program. It is difficult enough to accomplish this in those studies done in the English language, but we are going to encounter difficulties with important efforts written in other tongues (such as Diem in German, Pereira in Portuguese, and Van Schagen in French, to mention just a few). Fortunately, the recently published history of Indian physical education written by Rajagopalan is in English.

History of physical education and sport within education is a branch of educational history, and educational history is a branch of history. History of educational institutions, within the past decade at least, has achieved a certain amount of academic respectability, and we in physical education now have the opportunity to make a solid historical contribution, if we are but up to the task. At present we appear to be far from ready to meet this opportunity and responsibility. It is the unfortunate truth that we are too often busy attempting to make scholars out of activity-minded people who have never really become curious about the various aspects of our culture.

PHILOSOPHY OF PHYSICAL EDUCATION AND SPORT

That there has been an upsurge of interest in philosophy appears to be self-evident and needs very little substantiation.[3] Man's rapid progress in science,

---

[3] This material on philosophy was taken largely from a body of knowledge report presented by this writer to the Western Conference Physical Education Directors Meeting at Iowa City, Iowa, December 9, 1965.

and his retrogression, or dubious progress, in the realm of dubious affairs, have forced intelligent men and women everywhere to take stock. Unfortunately, it is next to impossible to gain historical perspective on the rapid change that is taking place, and a seemingly unprecedented burden has been imposed on man's understanding of himself and his world. Everywhere, therefore, we see a need for research, and then for more research. With all of this research endeavor, then, the rate of scientific and technological progress accelerates, and it is all becoming an "exciting but vicious circle." One wonders whether this pace can continue, because research has a way of multiplying questions much faster than we can ever hope to answer them. The question may well be asked if we have already exceeded our ability to assimilate the research findings that are being reported daily, and who can answer this question? Certainly it is true that our knowledge about the physical fields and the biological processes has vastly exceeded the development of fundamental knowledge about human behavior. Eventually someone, or some group, is going to have to decide to what extent further research in particular directions should be supported financially. Can we "manage this whole affair" in such a way that wise and intelligent decisions will be made in the light of the many scientific findings, and in such a way that "the good life," whatever that may be, will be available to all men on earth? Man must learn quickly to employ and direct science in the best possible way to serve humanity. Thus enters the question of the values by which men live, and we have come full circle to explain the upsurge of interest in philosophy.

A study covering literature which has a relationship, no matter how tenuous, to the philosophy of physical education and sport could conceivably run into hundreds of pages, and this would never do. On the other hand, if a discussion were presented about only those studies which employed the structural analysis technique of philosophical research, this phase of the volume at hand would be noticeably brief. Obviously, a compromise is necessary. This discussion, therefore, limits itself to providing some of the answers to two questions: 1) What is the philosophic task?; and 2) How may philosophical investigation be related to physical education and sport activities? A third question—What studies have been conducted in this field along philosophical lines during the past three decades?—will be left to the end of each historical treatment of the various persistent problems (and all of these studies are included in the general bibliography at the end of the book).

the philosophic task

Probably there are as many definitions of the philosophic task as there are philosophers; hence, no effort will be made to be all-inclusive. Furthermore, any attempt to gain consensus on this point is automatically doomed to failure. The safest approach for any quasi-philosopher is simply to state at the outset that his opinions about the philosophic task are his own—that they have been developed from his personal background reading and experience, and from his association with others of like interest.

Proceeding from this premise, it can be said that this writer sees philosophers as scholars dedicated to, and perhaps ultimately responsible for, the outlook and values of the various societies and cultures in which they live. Still further, the philosopher attempts to evaluate what we know and believe about the universe and our own sphere of human affairs. Subsequently he may evolve a systematic and coherent plan by which a human being may live. Following this, he may attempt to justify his position in various ways against other competing philosophical approaches. In the process he may analyze these other positions carefully; he may make comparisons; and he may show what he believes to be their deficiencies. It is conceivable that he may gradually, or even suddenly, change his own position because of cumulative scientific evidence which appears to refute what he had previously held to be true. Finally, he may even abandon the traditional or "scientific" approaches to philosophizing completely, if he becomes convinced that up to now it hasn't been possible "to be clear about exactly what we are saying or even exactly what the question is that we are asking" (Hospers, 1953, xii).

Up to this point, therefore, we have said that the philosopher may approach his work *speculatively, normatively,* or *analytically.* He may speculate about what we know and believe about the universe and our own sphere of human affairs within this framework. He may approach these questions normatively and evolve a systematic and coherent plan whereby a human may live. He may seek to analyze other philosophical approaches critically and to make comparisons. In this latter approach he will probably attempt to clarify concepts and to present evidence that seems to bear out one position or the other. Finally, he may go so far with critical analysis that he will decide that language analysis and semantics should be his primary task.

The difference between the traditional philosophic method and the scientific method should be made clear. Rather than aiming at a solution of a limited number of the factors and variables through rigid experimental control, the philosophic method attempts instead to include every factor or variable that is either directly or remotely relevant to the problem. In this way an effort is made to arrive at "a synthesis which is not only consistent with the best current data but also with the best experience drawn from the past." As Brubacher makes clear (Third Edition, 1962, p. 6), "...philosophy itself uncovers no new facts. It processes the facts of other disciplines but owns none of its own."

The philosophy of physical, health, and recreation education is a subdivision of the philosophy of education, itself a subdivision of the whole discipline of philosophy. Let us see what the philosopher Frankena, who himself has evidenced a deep interest in both the philosophy of education and in language analysis, has to say about the subject matter of education:

> We come, thus, to the subject of education. What is it? Actually, the term "education" is ambiguous and may mean any one of four things:
> (1) the *activity of educating* carried on by teachers, schools, and parents (or by oneself),
> (2) the *process of being educated* (or learning) which goes on in the pupil or child,
> (3) the *result,* actual or intended, of (1) and (2),
> (4) the *discipline* or field of enquiry that studies or reflects on (1), (2), and (3) and is taught in schools of education. (Frankena, 1965, p. 6)

Writing in 1956, Frankena spoke about being able "to distinguish at least the outlines" of speculative, normative, and analytical philosophy of education. At that time he said, "Of these the first and second can now seem to belong to the philosophy of the process of education and the third to the philosophy of the discipline of education" (Frankena, 1956, p. 98). In his later writing, however, Frankena seems willing to include normative philosophy of education under the discipline of education when he states,

> The philosophy of education is part of the discipline of education as defined earlier. It may either be *analytical* or *normative*. It is normative insofar as it is concerned to propose ends or values for education to promote, principles for it to follow, excellences for it to foster, or methods, contents, programs, etc., for it to adopt or employ, in general or specific situations. It is analytical insofar as it is concerned merely to analyze, clarify, or elucidate, or to criticize and evaluate, our thinking about education—the concepts or terms we employ, the arguments we use, the assumptions we make, the slogans we proclaim, the theories we formulate. (Frankena, 1965, p. 8)

This statement would seem to indicate that Frankena still feels there is really a legitimate place in schools of education for normative philosophers of education (and physical education!) who write texts in which the aims, principles, and means of a particular educational position are delineated for those involved in the "activity of educating."

To the reader it may now be obvious that true philosophizing is a highly complex discipline that may be practiced adequately by a highly intelligent professional person. It should be equally clear that amateurs should "enter upon the scene carefully where angels fear to tread." For this reason it seems logical that philosophizing of a speculative nature (if practiced at all!) should be left to true experts.[4] To what extent educational philosophers (and physical education philosophers) should involve themselves with speculative philosophy is debatable, although there is no doubt that some educational philosophers do qualify for this type of endeavor. We should keep in mind, of course, that many "pure" philosophers have given up this aspect of the work because of what they feel is its futility. Where physical education philosophers fit into this picture at present is self-evident.

Physical educators may well ask if they have a place at all. The answer again seems to be self-evident—yes! But it stands to reason that the assumption of such a role should not be taken lightly—certainly not as lightly as it seems to have been taken in the past. Unless physical educators have adequate backgrounds in the discipline of philosophy (and philosophy of education), they should not be encouraged or allowed to select thesis topics in these areas. To be sure, these related departments would undoubtedly view the selection of advanced fifth- and sixth-year courses in their subject matter most unfavorably, if they would even allow such selection. In summary, therefore, *adequately prepared* physical educators ought to be able to approach the philos-

---

[4] This is not to say that any person, and especially a teacher, does not have the right, or the responsibility, to develop his own philosophy of life, religion, education, etc.

ophy of physical education and sport *normatively* and *analytically* and should do so increasingly in the future. The era in which the "scholarly" contributions to the philosophy of physical education were made by physical education leaders and administrators *with inadequate backgrounds in philosophy* is just about over. This is not to say that their statements won't be welcome, or that perhaps the rank and file of the profession won't pay greater heed to their words than those of the philosophy specialists, but well-informed professional physical educators will be forced to take into consideration the sources and the backgrounds from which these individuals speak. In any case, there is certainly a continuing need to train physical educators systematically and thoroughly so that they may undertake normative and analytical philosophical research of high quality.

relating philosophical investigation to physical education

At the present moment in North America, the field of physical, health, and recreation education is being affected by certain social influences which are so strong that it is almost "being swept along out of control by the fast-moving current." On the one hand, we are groping toward an understanding of the concept of internationalism in a shrinking world; in sharp contrast, there are also strong forces of a nationalistic nature at work driving our field into a position where it could conceivably be called "physical fitness" or even "sport" (in some people's eyes). The fact that acceptance of these terms as the primary function relegates the field to secondary status in the educational system, and in the hierarchy of values in our society, doesn't seem to be bothering many physical educators. Of course, many feel that this is where the field belonged anyhow, and it is just now finding its rightful place. The typical physical fitness advocate believes that young people (and adults!) are deficient in bodily musculature and endurance anyhow, and here is a way to start children early in life, exercise them vigorously, discipline them thoroughly, and thereby give them a sound physical base upon which intellectual competence can be superimposed.

There is one major difficulty with the approach of those who would raise physical fitness to such a paramount position in the program: rightly or wrongly, a considerable percentage of the male physical educators and coaches, and a still larger percentage of the women in the field, are not ready to accept all that such a physical fitness emphasis implies. This latter group believes that physical education is really education *through* the medium of the physical, and that there is no such thing as education *of* the physical—that the mind-body dichotomy is something from the past, long ago disproved by psychologists and others. The term "total fitness" means something to these people; they see health education, safety education, physical education, sport and athletics, dance, and recreation education as integral phases of the curriculum. The term "social intelligence" as defined by Dewey, or perhaps even the term "social self-realization" as stressed by Brameld, involves knowledges, competencies, and skills related to citizenship, personality traits, and moral values in the broadest sense.

On the one hand, therefore, the pendulum seems to be swinging sharply to the right in the direction of an essentialistic educational philosophy. The result is that many physical educators are searching rather frantically for a discipline involving a body of scientific knowledge that will bring, they hope, a certain amount of academic respectability to the field. Progressivists, because of their allegiance to the scientific method, can work hand in hand with all other discipline-seekers. The President's Council on Physical Fitness is striving for a much greater amount of vigorous physical training in our programs, and those who would venture the belief that physical *education* has a greater role to play in the educational process are challenged to produce substantial proof. Admittedly, this is quite difficult to do. But despite the advent of the Cold War and the Space Age, many educational leaders in our profession are standing by their beliefs that physical education does contribute to the educational process in many ways. It does seem to be true, however, that many important members of our lay public are siding, occasionally quite vociferously, with the rising tide of essentialism in education.

These current trends in the philosophy of physical, health, and recreation education, which undoubtedly are the result of conflicting philosophies of education in each of the fifty public educational systems extant in these United States, have perpetuated such a blurred image of the field that professional practitioners are typically quite confused. This confusion is often unconsciously transmitted to professional students, who find themselves at a loss when faced with a need to explain to parents and the general public what our field can and should do with the nation's children in the recommended daily program of physical education.

To understand how physical education and, for that matter, the entire educational structure got itself into this situation, we must look to our philosophical foundations. For the first time in the history of physical education, scholars have become truly aware of the need to turn to philosophy in an effort *to delineate the implications* for our subject of the leading philosophical tendencies of the Western world. (The fact that no consideration is being given here to philosophical movements in the Orient reaffirms pointedly the narrow provincialism of a world that is technologically shrinking day by day.) At least we have begun to apply philosophical concepts and methods of analysis directly to physical education and sport. This experiment, still in its infancy, is of mutual importance to both philosophy and physical education, for, pragmatically, philosophy must "bake bread," if it is to survive in our rapidly changing world.

Of late many people in our field have been using the word "philosophy" with increasing frequency. Currently there seems to be a "philosophy" of almost everything; for instance, a recently published article bore the title, "A Philosophy of Base Running"! This development shouldn't cause too much concern, since it points to a new awareness by our culture of the need for reassessment of its value system. Such awareness is heartening, but often quite superficial, because most individuals lack philosophical background. Furthermore, "actions speak louder than words"; one can undoubtedly learn more about a person's value system by observing his conduct than by listening to him describe his philosophical position, no matter how eloquent he may be. For those involved in teacher education, the task is to help the prospective teacher of physical education and sport understand his own philosophical position. Because backgrounds are so varied, very few, if any, can accept any one philosophical position (e.g., pragmatism) in its entirety. Most people seem to develop a type of "patterned eclecticism" that works for them. The teacher of philosophy has the age-old, intangible task, not of imparting knowledge about a specific "thing," but of educing self-examination. He can only hope that a reasonable amount of internal consistency will evolve in this "process of becoming."

brief historical background

Philosophy had its beginning in Greece over 2,500 years ago, where the word originally meant knowledge or love of wisdom. The first method to be used by philosophers was speculation, a method which many professional philosophers still employ today and which, interestingly enough, is an integral part of the scientific method first developed during the Renaissance. The ancients themselves in their search for a logical universe made a distinction between speculative knowledge and that practical knowledge gained through experience and observation. In the course of this "dialogue on method," three leading philosophic tendencies emerged—idealism, realism, and pragmatism. Of course, they were not known under these titles until the late nineteenth and early twentieth centuries. The influence of these schools of thought is still very strong in the 1960s, despite the inroads that have recently been made by language analysis and existentialism.

IDEALISM, which can be traced through Plato, the Hebrew-Christian tradition in religion, Descartes, Spinoza, Leibniz, Berkeley, and Kant to Hegel, postulates that man is a real, existent being with a soul; that in each man is a spirit or mind which is basically real; that the essence of the entire universe is mind or spirit; and that man is a son of God, who created the universe.

REALISM (or NOMINALISM), which got its start with Aristotle and developed through the philosophical thought of St. Thomas Aquinas, Descartes, Comenius, Spinoza, Locke, Kant, Herbart, James, and the various schools of the twentieth century, implies that man lives in a world which is undoubtedly real; that things actually happen exactly the way man experiences them; that man's experience does not change any knowledge that may enter into his consciousness; that things are just the same as they were before such experience occurred; and that reality "out there" is independent of man's mind.

PRAGMATISM may be said to have begun with Heraclitus; gathered momentum with Francis Bacon and John Locke; gained strength through the many early scientists of the sixteenth and seventeenth centuries; and blossomed into fruition through Comte, Peirce, James, and Dewey. Its position is that the world is *constantly* changing; that an idea is not true until it is tested through experience; that we can only learn what an idea really *means* by putting it into practice; and that we can't ever really discover the nature of the universe.

It is most difficult to gain historical perspective on the philosophical trends and developments of the past one hundred years. It is apparent, however, that there have been strong attacks on many of the traditional approaches described above. Prior to World War I, idealism had lost some of the prestige it had enjoyed in the late 1800s. The defense of scientific investigation by Spencer and Darwin was a tremendously powerful influence. Pragmatism continued to be influential, especially in the United States. It gathered much strength from naturalism and from the rise of the spirit of scientific inquiry. Great emphasis was placed on the desirability of testing hypotheses through experience in order to gain "true" knowledge.

PHILOSOPHICAL ANALYSIS, a development of the past forty years, attempts to provide an answer to the recurring question, "What is philosophical knowledge?" Developing scientific method has forced many of today's philosophers to ask themselves, "In what kind of activity am I engaging? Does philosophical activity result in knowledge after all?" If true knowledge can come only from scientific experimentation, what is the justification for philosophy? A considerable group of influential people within the discipline of philosophy feel that, since knowledge must be communicable, *philosophy's primary function is to use language terms clearly and correctly.*

EXISTENTIALISM is still another type of philosophizing that has emerged as a significant force during the past one hundred years. This approach started as a revolt against Hegel's idealism, which held that ethical and spiritual realities were accessible to man through reason. One sector developed the position which affirmed that man's task was to create his own ideals and values. According to Nietzsche, science had shown that the transcendent ideals of the Church were nonsense—"God is dead." Thus man is "on his own" in a cold, cruel world. Man, spelled with a capital "M," is the only one who can give meaning and direction to a world lacking in these qualities. Can he so direct and guide his own existence that responsible social action will result? This is the fundamental question.

What *is* the answer to the many philosophical questions about the nature of the world, the problem of good and evil, the possibility of free will, the existence of God, the greater importance of some values as opposed to others, the possibility of man's really acquiring knowledge, and the nature of beauty —just to name a few of life's enigmas? It is safe to say that no one person or group has the answers organized in such form that anything close to universal acceptance would result.

EDUCATIONAL PHILOSOPHY, really a subdivision of philosophy, devotes itself to an analysis of the implications from the various philosophical positions for three major areas: 1) the relationships among society, school, and the individual; 2) educational aims and objectives; and 3) the process of education. More specifically, questions have been asked (and partially answered) relative to standardization of instruction, administrative control, teacher control, the psychology of learning, the definition of subject matter, the role of measurement and evaluation, the aims of the process of education, the importance of interest in learning, the need for indoctrination and discipline, and many others.

For some time the writer has been recommending that philosophy, and specifically educational philosophy, has true meaning for us in physical, health, and recreation education, if we will only make the effort to comprehend our philosophical foundations (Zeigler, 1964, and other papers listed in the General Bibliography). This approach won't give us the answers to all our problems overnight, but such analysis will place us in a much better position to meet our persistent, recurring historical problems intelligently *when we know where we stand*; and we can then discuss conflicting philosophies more logically and consistently than we have been able to do up to this time.

Investigators in the Graduate Department of Physical Education at Illinois are currently developing a unique approach to the history, philosophy, and administrative theory of physical education and sport. In the field of history, for example, some fourteen persistent problems have been identified as follows: 1) values; 2) the influence of politics; 3) the influence of nationalism; 4) the influence of economics; 5) the influence of religion; 6) professional preparation; 7) methods of instruction; 8) the role of administration; 9) the healthy body; 10) physical education and recreation for women; 11) dance in physical education and recreation; 12) the use of leisure; 13) amateur, semi-professional, and professional athletics; and 14) the concept of progress.

In relation to the philosophy of physical education and sport, the assumption has been made that physical educators with an adequate background in philosophy and philosophy of education ought to be able to philosophize normatively and analytically about their field in regard to its place in education and in society. An attempt is being made, therefore, to delineate the implications for our subject of the leading philosophical tendencies of the Western world. Thus, pragmatism, realism, idealism, philosophy of language, and existentialism have been subsumed to relatively corresponding tendencies in educational philosophy, such as experimentalism (pragmatic naturalism), reconstructionism, romantic naturalism, naturalistic realism, rational humanism, Catholic moderate realism, and idealism. Philosophy of language is being treated as philosophy "in a new key," and existentialism is conceived of as a "flavoring" influence.

The assumption has been made that philosophical analysis of the persistent historical problems will enable professional practitioners to realize the need for ordered, consistent, and logical personal philosophies. A consistent philosophy of administration, for example, will give direction to those administering programs in this field—direction that is sorely needed as we wait for the developing social science of administration to outline the most effective way to manage organizations. Here the objective has been to apply current administrative theory, based largely on the research conducted in public administration, business administration, educational administration, and the behavioral sciences. Our hope is that an analysis of the theoretical frameworks used in administrative research will enable us to develop our own unique theoretical framework for administration in the field of physical education and competitive athletics.

For all these reasons, the many graduate faculties in physical education are urged to develop a coordinated approach to scholarly and research endeavor in the history, philosophy, and administrative theory of physical education and sport. The greatest possible good would result if these areas, and others related to the humanities and social sciences, received an emphasis comparable to that of the natural sciences. Our overall goal is to discover what contributions physical, health, and recreation education can make to the development of man, to what extent society will accept this evidence, and how we may best administer those programs of this type which are offered within the framework of general education.

CONCLUDING STATEMENT

In this chapter we have presented what is felt to be a primary need in our field now and in the future. It is a truism to state that we need a much stronger body of knowledge based on orderly and coordinated research so that we may eventually, and hopefully soon, call ourselves a fine profession. We have developed professional preparation that is intellectual in character; we are service-oriented; and we are not judged to be successful by the size of our bank accounts. Furthermore, we have a code of ethics (the enforcement of which, unfortunately, is rarely tested); we have certain public recognition (the level of which could undoubtedly be higher); we have professional leaders who are devoting their entire lives to the task; we are acquiring definite performance skills; and we have a fellowship with our associates through various meetings and published literature. Despite these dramatic advances, there still remains the basic need for an organized body of knowledge based on legitimate research—and this is certainly true in the areas of history and philosophy. Those of us involved in professional preparation can make decisions about who goes on this "difficult road" of scholarly and research endeavor. It is up to us to give bright young students the lead, to indicate to them where they should go, what they are after, how they may obtain it, and possibly what they can do with it then. After that it is up to them. We can draw a "rough" blueprint for the cooperative research effort that will give us the body of knowledge that we need so desperately. "And so we had better strive to become clearly and fully conscious of who we are, where we are, how we got this way," and which path we should take (Muller, 1952, p. 33).

> Two roads diverged in a wood, and I—
> I took the one less traveled by, —
> And that has made all the difference.   (Robert Frost)

REFERENCES

As we move forward to a consideration of some eleven persistent problems selected for consideration in this volume, the reader is urged to consider his own background in history and philosophy generally, and in the history and philosophy of education specifically. This brief volume can stand on its own, but by its very length it can't help but be relatively superficial in the consideration of such vast subject matters. The following short list of selected references can be invaluable for supplementary reading and browsing:

1. Brubacher, John S. *A History of the Problems of Education* (2nd ed.). New York: McGraw-Hill Book Co., 1966.

2. ————. *Modern Philosophies of Education* (3rd ed.). New York: McGraw-Hill Book Co., 1962.

3. Butler, J. Donald. *Four Philosophies* (rev. ed.). New York: Harper & Row, Publishers, 1957.

4. Kaplan, Abraham. *The New World of Philosophy*. New York: Random House, 1961.

5. McNeill, William H. *The Rise of the West*. Chicago: The University of Chicago Press, 1963.

6. Meyerhoff, H. ed. *The Philosophy of History in Our Time*. New York: Doubleday & Company, Inc., 1959.

7. Morris, Van Cleve. *Philosophy and the American School*. Boston: Houghton Mifflin Company, 1961.

8. Muller, Herbert J. *The Uses of the Past*. New York: The New American Library of World Literature, Inc., 1954.

9. Woody, Thomas. *Life and Education in Early Societies*. New York: The Macmillan Company, 1949.

10. Zeigler, Earle F. *Philosophical Foundations for Physical, Health, and Recreation Education*. Englewood Cliffs, N.J.: Prentice-Hall, Inc., 1964.

II

Values in Physical Education
and Sport

Perhaps the most persistent problem that the physical, health, and recreation education teacher faces is the determination of his educational values, and how his particular subject matter contributes to the achievement of these values in the lives of his students. If certain values are available through instruction, then sincere teachers will obviously aim to bring about the realization of these values. Such values become the aims of education and, somewhat more narrowly, the aims of physical, health, and recreation education. The plan of this book is to help the teacher realize his underlying set of personal values so that he will pursue his profession with a reasonable degree of consistency.

In order to answer the question of what educational values derive from physical, health, and recreation education, we must first consider some fundamental questions. Then we proceed to trace the various historical aims in accordance with these values.[1]

An examination of the diagram explaining philosophy and its branches will indicate that *axiology*, the fourth subdivision, is the end result of philosophizing. The individual must develop a system of values consistent with his beliefs in the other three subdivisions. Some believe that values exist only because of the interest of the valuer (*the interest theory*). *The existence theory*, conversely, holds that values exist independently. According to this theory man's task is to discover the "real"

---

[1] At this point, the reader should turn to Appendices A and B at the back of the book. Follow the instructions given for the professional checklist and attempt to determine your own philosophical stance. After reading Appendix B carefully, note that it would be very difficult to employ the existentialistic position within the framework of the professional checklist.

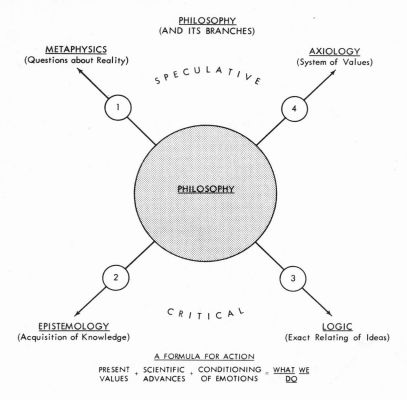

PHILOSOPHY
(AND ITS BRANCHES)

METAPHYSICS
(Questions about Reality)

AXIOLOGY
(System of Values)

S P E C U L A T I V E

1

4

PHILOSOPHY

2

3

C R I T I C A L

EPISTEMOLOGY
(Acquisition of Knowledge)

LOGIC
(Exact Relating of Ideas)

A FORMULA FOR ACTION

$$\frac{PRESENT}{VALUES} + \frac{SCIENTIFIC}{ADVANCES} + \frac{CONDITIONING}{OF\ EMOTIONS} = \frac{WHAT\ WE}{DO}$$

values—to give existence to their ideal essence. *The experimentalist theory* explains value somewhat differently; values which yield results that have "cash value" bring about the possibility of greater happiness through more effective values in the future. One further theory, *the part-whole theory*, postulates that effective relating of parts to the whole brings about the highest values.

Axiology itself has various domains. First and foremost, we must consider *ethics*, which has to do with morality, conduct, good and evil, and ultimate objectives in life. There are several approaches to the problem of whether life, as we know it, is worthwhile. A person who goes around all the time with a smile on his face looking hopefully toward the future is, of course, an optimist (*optimism*). Some people become easily discouraged and wonder if life is worth the struggle (*pessimism*). In between these two extremes we find the golden mean, *meliorism* (from the Latin, *better*), which implies that an individual constantly strives to improve his situation. This position assumes that man can't make any final decisions about whether good or evil will prevail in the world.

Perhaps the key question to be considered in ethics is, "What is the purpose of *my* existence?" Under this heading we encounter the belief that pleasure is the highest good (*hedonism*). One approach that has developed in modern history from hedonistic doctrine is *utilitarianism.* Society, not the individual, is the focus, since the basic idea is to promote the greatest happiness for the greatest number of people in the community. Although the utilitarian recognizes the existence of various types of pleasure (ranging from intense, momentary emotional pleasure to the pleasure reflected in a placid life of contentment), he believes that seeking this type of pleasure will fulfill his own moral duty. Another important way of looking at the summum bonum (or highest good) in life is called *perfectionism.* Here the individual is aiming for complete self-realization and accordingly envisions a society of self-fulfilled individuals.

A logical outcome of an individual's decision about the greatest good in life is the standard of conduct he sets for himself. Certain interests are apt to guide our conduct in life. If we are too self-centered, people will say that we are egotistical (*egoism*). Some people go to the other extreme; they feel that a person best fulfills himself when he plays down the realization of his own interests in order to serve society or some social group therein (*altruism*). Once again, Aristotle's concept of the "golden mean" comes to the fore as a workable solution to this question.

One of the other areas of value under axiology deals with the "feeling" aspects of man's conscious life (*aesthetics*). Aesthetics, the philosophy of taste, asks whether there are principles which govern the search for the beautiful in life. Because there has been a need to define still further values in the life of man, we now have specialized philosophies of education and religion. Further, we often refer to a man's social philosophy, which simply means that men make decisions about values intrinsic to various institutions, *e.g.,* the educational process.[2]

ARE VALUES OBJECTIVE OR SUBJECTIVE?

Now that we have a brief overview of the question of values, the individual should ask himself whether he believes values are objective or subjective; that is, do values exist whether man is present to realize them or not? Or is it man who ascribes value to his various relationships with other people and his physical environment? If a physical education program fulfills aims and objectives *inherently* valuable to youth, then it should be included in the curriculum whether students or parents recognize this value or not. If, on the other hand, it were proved that physical education has relatively little value, that the majority of persons sees no need for it, then according to the subjective theory of value it should be eliminated.

Another facet of the question of values relates to their qualitative aspects. Some things in life are desired by the individual, whereas others may be desirable mainly because society has indicated its approval of them. A continuous appraisal of values occurs. If a value exists in and for itself, it is

---

[2] For further reading on this subject, the student should consult J. Donald Butler, *Four Philosophies* (rev. ed.). (New York: Harper & Row, Publishers, Inc., 1957), pp. 48–54.

said to be an intrinsic value. One that serves as a means to an end, however, has become known as an instrumental value. When intense emotion and appreciation are involved, this gradation of value is called aesthetic. Physical education offers many opportunities to realize such aesthetic values, although many well-educated people view physical, health, and recreation education far too narrowly and thereby confine aesthetic values to experiences in the fine arts and literature.

A HIERARCHY OF EDUCATIONAL VALUES

Every culture seeks to develop its own hierarchy of educational values. In our own society certain essentialistic philosophies of education, which hold that educational values are objective, encourage the gradation of these given values. Further, the disciplines at the top of their value-hierarchy are those involving reason. If such values seem to coincide with eternal values inherent in the universe itself, they are considered still more valuable and are rated even more highly. So-called instrumental (pragmatic) values, conversely, are typically ranked much lower on the scale. Thus, physical, health, and recreation education might well be considered important by the idealist, but it would not take precedence over another subject which seemingly invokes man's rational powers to a greater extent, and which would thereby help him achieve still "higher" goals in his life.

To the experimentalist (as a progressivist), on the other hand, competency in, *e.g.*, self-defense or survival swimming might on a given occasion rate at the very top of the educational hierarchy—especially if such competency were necessary to save a life in an emergency. Thus, there is no question but that the role of physical, health, and recreation education in the educational pattern will vary depending on the final or ultimate aims of education to which the individual subscribes. Specific educational objectives in such situations would have to be chosen in the light of these ultimate goals.

With this introduction we are now ready to survey the aims and objectives of our specialized field as evidenced in the value systems, and hence in the educational systems, of various societies throughout recorded history.

PHYSICAL CULTURE IN EARLY SOCIETIES

primitive and preliterate society

In primitive society there appears to have been very little organized, purposive instruction in physical education; education was usually incidental, a by-product of daily experience. The daily activities of labor, searching for food, dancing, and games were essential to the development of superior bodies and to survival. In addition to promoting physical efficiency, these activities helped strengthen membership in the society and served as a means of recreation.

Egypt

Physical education in early Egypt was not part of any formal educational system; rather, it was simply instrumental in completing daily work activities. The development of certain social institutions had influenced the types of physical activity engaged in by people of different social classes, either through direction or by choice. The upper class received educational advantages not available to others. Sports and dancing were popular with the nobility, but such opportunities were limited even for them except during times of religious observances or when the inundation of the Nile took place.

The masses in Egypt had to master a variety of physical skills to earn their livelihood. These were acquired through varying types of apprenticeship, such as weaving or nail-making. When the Nile flooded even the masses got relief from life's typical heavy labor and could take part in leisure activities. As was often the case throughout history, fishing, hunting, and fowling were engaged in for pleasure by some and as business by many. Furthermore, pictorial evidence of all sorts of games abounds, especially the kind played by children and youth.

When the army became a distinct class of society, men acquired physical skills that prepared them to do battle. There were all sorts of military exercises and maneuvers that would prepare young men to use a bow, to wield a battle-axe, and to hurl a lance. Wrestling was a most popular activity, and many evidently acquired a fairly high degree of skill. Swimming became a common skill as well. Some persons became so proficient that they can be designated as professionals—the soldier, of course, but also professional dancers, acrobats, wrestlers, and bullfighters. It can also be assumed that many people engaged in sports for the sheer pleasure it gave them. This tends to correct an earlier impression, probably accepted erroneously from the really sport-conscious Greeks, that the Egyptians were actually not concerned with such pursuits to any extent at all.

Babylon and Assyria

These cultures were quite similar to that of Egypt in their development of social institutions. Thus, the physical activity available was usually appropriate to the station of the individual concerned. Workmen taught their trades to their sons. Women did the household work, and their daughters learned how to fulfill the same function through informal apprenticeship. Not much information is available about possible sports and recreational activities for the lower classes, although there must have been occasional opportunities for dancing, music, informal games, and rudimentary hunting and fishing. We do know, for example, that fishing was usually a regulated business rather than an idle pastime.

One chief business was the fighting of wars, and this meant that soldiers in training received a great deal of physical training along these lines. The infantry was usually composed of soldiers from the lower classes, while the charioteers and horsemen possessed greater social status. Archers were said to have come from the mountainous areas.

the early Hebrews

For the early Hebrews there was again really no organized physical training and sport; physical culture was demanded for the purpose of military defense primarily. Certain health safeguards, *e.g.,* dietary regulations and the promotion of cleanliness, were looked upon as religious obligations. Wholesome activities were promoted especially on the Sabbath—"a time for recreation of mind and body; but idleness was condemned." (Woody, 1949, p. 106)

China

In the ancient Chinese civilization, formal physical education had little if any place. The major aim was to preserve and perpetuate the existing social order—an order which could only be classified as nonprogressive. Even the military motive, present in the other early cultures, was nonexistent here. As a type of classical civilization evolved and various religious influences were felt, even less emphasis was placed on physical development. Health standards were poor indeed. In later Chinese history, soldiers received military training. Judging by the nature of the combat, this was definitely rigorous.

With all the emphasis on academic excellence, there appears to have been little understanding of the possibility of using physical recreation to relieve intellectual strain. In the early times it is true, however, that sons in the upper-class families did have an opportunity to learn dancing, and then later on, as young men, they received instruction in archery and charioteering. At the beginning of the third millennium, an early emperor, Fu Hi, evidently encouraged his subjects to hunt and fish and saw to it that they received instruction.

India

Although India has typically been known as the "sickest nation in the world," and although the climate and the religious philosophy forced a certain rejection of physical activity, there does appear to be evidence that the matter of individual and communal health received considerable attention in ancient times. Hygienic rules and ritualistic dances in accordance with religious beliefs were common among the Hindus. Archeological finds point out that many sports and amusements were part of the early life, and the early Vedic hymns praised such attributes as strength, health, and bravery. There is no doubt that soldiers, farmers, and artisans engaged in strenuous physical activity as part of their occupations, and there is continued mention of the importance of proper diet. The primitive Aryan conquerors, on the other hand, were not concerned about the health and physical training of the populace.

Much later, Buddha himself is said to have neglected "manly exercises"; his prohibitions against exercises and games indicate that people typically took part in all sorts of games, tumbling, wrestling, boxing, swordsmanship, and riding. The unique Indian practice of Yoga has continued from ancient times down to the present day and involves systematic exercises in posture, stretching, and breathing—an interrelationship of mind and body in which fifteen "postures" are still commonly accepted today.

Still further, the horse, the war chariot, archery, wrestling, and a chivalrous code of conduct are referred to on numerous occasions in early Vedic and later literature. Later a more distinct warrior class was established, of which there were six subdivisions under one governing body. One army, for example, was said to have numbered as high as 400,000, and was composed of admiralty, transport, infantry, cavalry, war chariots, and elephants.

Iran

The Persians developed an admirable educational tradition, in keeping, of course, with the mores and customs of the time. Moral training in obedience and truthfulness was inculcated by the wise men of the society. However, this education, provided only for the children of the upper-class families, totally neglected literary and general intellectual attainment.

The three major classes in Persian society were priests, soldiers, and tradesmen. The latter received a type of "physical culture" through apprenticeship in farming, trade, and mechanics. The soldiers, of course, received careful and thorough training at arms. According to Herodotus, boys had to know the fundamentals of horsemanship and archery, and throwing the javelin was also an essential skill in this militaristic society. Other elements of training which assumed significant importance were hunting (from prehistoric times of great value in all early societies), wrestling and hand-to-hand combat, the events of the Pentathlon, and polo (or chugan, as it was called).

Crete

In this island culture hunting with the bow and arrow seems to have been prominent and very popular. Bull-grappling was also a well-developed art or profession, in which women and men engaged while performing fantastic gymnastic maneuvers. Wrestling and boxing are depicted on artifacts, as are various types of gladiatorial contests. There appears also to have been a sacral quality to some sports, as more commonly pertained to music and dancing. The fact that the Cretans were surrounded by water means that they had to learn to swim; and some remains show evidence of the breaststroke and an overhand sidestroke with a flutter kick of a type. There is disagreement as to whether Cretans took part in or were influenced by Greece's great athletic festivals. As yet, however, there is no evidence that organized training in sport existed.

Greece

There is universal recognition of the fact that physical education was highly valued in ancient Greek society. From 1100 to 700 B.C., the Homeric Age, athletic sports held a prominent place in the culture. As a society of individualists, the Greeks sought to develop physical *and* intellectual excellence in their citizens—to produce a man of action.

SPARTA.   The goal of Spartan society was the development of devoted citizens and fine soldiers. Obviously, physical training was the chief educational tool. Young Spartans' training was exactly what one might expect—a strict regimen, firm discipline, and most strenuous activity, all designed eventually to produce a hardy, courageous young man. When the exercise program was in session, everyone was expected to be active at all times.

It is noteworthy that specialization in competitive athletics was not encouraged. This was especially true if it tended to interfere with the primary goal of turning out hardened, seasoned warriors. However, games and exercises which would contribute to the basic goal, such as wrestling, boxing, pancration, archery, hunting, riding, and other similar activities, were not lacking. Running, especially the race with full armor, had an important place in the training regimen. It was in these activities that the Spartans excelled at the Olympian games on numerous occasions.

ATHENS.   Harmonious development of body, mind, and spirit was of paramount concern to Athenians, and this is the first time in recorded history that physical education was valued so highly in the development of the ideal man. Although we tend to forget that these opportunities were designated for freemen only, we still remain astounded by the degree to which Athenian society did succeed in producing the "all-around" citizen.

The physical education of boys took place in a palaestra, an institution for wrestling and gymnastic activities, which was typically private and probably frequented by the sons of well-to-do families in the afternoons. It is possible that some sort of a rotational scheme was devised to keep the facilities in use during the daylight hours. These structures, supervised by trainers called paidotribes, were more or less elaborate depending on the economic status of the particular community in which they were built. The boys were divided into age groups and received training in exercise, games, diet, posture, combative sports, and track and field events. There is evidence that swimming and dancing, at least for some, were integral parts of the curriculum.

After the period at the palaestra, probably concluding with the fifteenth year, the sons of the wealthier families received competitive athletic instruction in the various public gymnasia. Since these were public facilities, however, it is quite likely that the more gifted warranted special attention despite their financial status. Training in warfare skills, and dancing for those involved in the chorus and other religious festivals, was stressed. A point of interest is that the paidotribe may be compared to today's general physical educator, while the gymnast, often a specialist, may be likened to our coach, a man who becomes more proficient in the development of a boy or young man in a specific sport or gymnastic activity. The director of the gymnasium was known as a gymnasiarch, usually a man of wealth performing a public service. It was his responsibility to supervise and to train athletes for special festivals, and he also directed the work of the various lesser officials and "maintenance men" of the gymnasium.

When training at the Ephebic College was added to the culture, a training that appears to have been informal in nature before it received official status in the fourth century, it was instituted for young men between the ages of eighteen and twenty. It appears that this training became compulsory and state-organized only after the defeat at Chaeronaea by the Macedonians in 338 B.C. The society could no longer allow itself the luxury of a militia characterized by individual freedom; instead its young citizens had to prepare to staff the patrolling units and the fortresses. The young men learned how to fight in battle armor and how to employ the spear, javelin, bow, and catapult. Undoubtedly, such activities as running, boxing, wrestling, swimming, horse riding, chariot-driving, and various types of forced marches were included in the training regimen. It has been argued that the Macedonians were professional soldiers, and the Greeks soon learned that their "amateur" soldiers could no longer compete on even terms. This must have been a painful period for the Athenians—a period in which they learned the hard way that their idealistic educational aim had to be subverted in the face of an impending encounter with highly trained opponents supported by improved technology of warfare.

The Greeks recognized sports and games for many reasons. From a realistic standpoint, they knew that these activities served a utilitarian purpose—preparation for the very important business of war. In addition, there is evidence that they understood full well that strenuous training developed strength, power, and endurance. They realized also that it was possible to stave off some of the effects of growing old by continuing to "play the game." Thus, the relationship between physical culture and vigorous health was apparent to them. Furthermore, the men of letters and those with creative artistic talents praised the realization of many of the innate drives of men which led them to aspire to noble words and deeds. And the various sociological and physical factors of the culture and geography combined to produce a vigorous, active life. Mortal men envisioned the gods they created as possessing these desired traits to the highest degree; so they tried to imitate their gods, and they praised them through the medium of athletic contests and festivals while honoring their own dead simultaneously. All types of festivals developed, which included a wide range of religious, artistic, and sporting activities. The Great Panathenaea games, for instance, celebrated the earlier unification of Attica under the city-state of Athens and were held for an eight-day period every four years. The legendary Olympic Games, the most famous of the Panhellenic festivals, were presumably first held in 776 B.C. at Olympia, a sacred spot in Ellis on the River Alpheus.

The great importance of the games and festivals in Greek life, the early amateur ideal, the gradual change in the character of the events through professional influence, and the eventual excesses of the worst type which entered the scene are quite well known to most readers and cannot be discussed at length here. That the changing political scene exercised a direct effect on the character of the games appears to be self-evident, a point that cannot be overemphasized. The national games of Greece served the people's religious needs; they helped the Greeks realize their kinship with one another; they aided them in the pursuit of excellence; and they provided these fascinating ancients with release, fun, and excitement.

Rome

PHYSICAL TRAINING AND EDUCATION.   There is evidence that children in the early Roman culture had all sorts of games to play and that these games were employed to serve ends other than play as the children grew older. Although the well-known *mens sana in corpore sano* is Latin, it does not express the Roman ideal—to prepare a citizen to bear arms for his nation, not to promote a harmonious development of spirit, mind, and body (as had been the case in Athens). The same basically natural activities were employed in this society as in all of the others described previously—they ran, jumped, hunted, boxed, wrestled, rode horseback, and learned to use the tools of war. Both boys and girls learned to swim, but dancing and music had little if any place, except occasionally in religious and public celebrations, such as triumphs of war. Competitive sports were limited largely to games that prepared for war. It is true that the circus games were early introduced into Roman life, but they were never carried to an excess—even broadly speaking—until the later days of the Republic.

A vigorous life was encouraged for many by the hard work on the farms and the subsequent military training. The Romans were most certainly warlike, strong, aggressive, courageous, durable, and well-disciplined; and their ability as warriors increased as they learned from experience. While the Romans did adopt much from the Hellenic culture, they never seemed to capture the spirit of the Greek athletic contests. One obvious reason for this is that the glory of the earlier athletic festivals had undoubtedly degenerated by the time the Romans conquered Greece, and the practical-minded victors couldn't envision any benefit to be derived from such activities. When they became "city folk," however, toward the end of the Republic, palaestras and gymnasia appeared in increasing number. The gradually increasing importance of such facilities may be noted thereafter throughout the days of the Empire.

Subsequently, Roman emperors built magnificent public baths and provided all sorts of extravagant games and entertainment to gain the approval of the populace. But, despite these developments, the Roman intellectual leaders took every opportunity to mock and repudiate the Greek system of active participation in gymnastics, music, and dancing. The Romans understood that man should be restless and active and that such activity contributed to the individual's health and strength; in fact, Cicero, Sallust, and Quintilian all stressed the utility of physical exercise. They were simply unwilling to grant it a respectable status in Roman education and may well have equated it with the degeneracy they saw taking place. Seneca indeed strikes a harsh blow at physical education; his advice was to exercise rapidly, get tired, and return to the more important aspects of life.

Many historians do affirm, however, that the Romans were strongly interested in recreation and play. This was probably more true before their wealth increased, when individual freedom was at its height and the military demands of the Empire nonexistent. It could be argued, of course, that the urge to play is an innate need for re-*creation* and refreshment present in all men. In any case, the Romans enjoyed various games, both of an active and a sedentary nature. Gambling was extremely popular, especially with the wealthy classes, and there were all sorts of games similar to chess and checkers. Ball games were played by all classes, but, strangely enough, the idea of striking a ball with a stick or racket does not seem to have gained acceptance to any considerable extent. They did have a number of differently sized balls and admired ambidextrous performers. Swimming and boating were popular recreations and often served a utilitarian purpose as well. Hunting and fishing were work for some and play for others—a distinction previously noted in other early societies.

The relationship of exercise to health was recognized by the Romans and should be discussed briefly here. Rome's geography seems to have invited disease and epidemics. And when the hardy, vigorous life of the early Republic gave way to the luxury of the Empire, degeneration set in. Romans' eating habits, for example, grew worse steadily, and their diseases seemed to have become much more complex. Celsus and Galen, physicians of the day, recognized the need for "medical gymnastics" and devised extensive remedial systems. Scorning the experience of the Greeks, they developed specializations of their own, of which a great deal was quackery. Eventually, though, improved community health services were made available. Early medical science did make significant progress despite the hindrances posed by charlatans and the so-called "saint cures" promulgated by the Christian and Gnostic sects.

The story of Rome's decline, its disastrous misuse of leisure, the passion for degrading entertainment that developed, and the horrible examples of man's inhumanity to man and his cruelty to beasts do not need reiteration. Did these excesses bring about the decline of Rome, or were they symptomatic of a declining Rome? At any rate, two factors should be obvious: the type and extent of physical education programs was dependent on the political system, and changing political and social conditions produced a culture which could not cope with its leisure time. These developments should be of interest to us in America today.

THE MIDDLE AGES

the "Dark Ages"

The Visigoths began their successful invasion to the south in 376 A.D., and the end of the Roman Empire is commonly dated at 476 A.D. The period following has been typically, but perhaps incorrectly, designated as the "Dark Ages," a time when most literature and learning came to a standstill and would have been completely lost save for the newly organized monasteries. "Ill blows the wind that profits nobody" is a proverb that applies to this era. The Visigoths did possess splendid bodies, and it is often argued that it was just this addition of "new blood" which made possible the development of the later medieval and Renaissance cultures.

Christian influence on physical education

As the immoral society of the declining Romans became a mere memory, Christianity continued to spread because of the energy, enthusiasm, and high moral standards of its followers. The Church managed to survive the invasion of the barbarians, gradually became an important influence in society, and continued to expand on all fronts. Although Jesus Christ was in many ways anything but an ascetic, the early Christians envisioned the individual's moral regeneration as the highest goal. They became most concerned about their souls and possible eternal happiness. The physical was of this world, and consequently evil; affairs of the soul were of God. This way of life, known as asceticism, saw the summum bonum in subduing the desires of the flesh, even by means of torture if necessary. Most churchmen were opposed to the idea of physical activity in sport and games because the Roman sports and games had led to so many evils and excesses, and also because athletic festivals had been associated with the earlier pagan religion. Further historical investigation is needed on this subject, however, as certain Catholic historians and educators have stated that the Church has been unjustly maligned on this point. Professor H. I. Marrou makes it quite clear that, in his opinion, physical education "simply died of old age." He maintains that it was the above-mentioned "passion for athletics" that was criticized so sharply (1964, p. 185).

And so for hundreds of years during this period of the early Middle Ages, there was no training or cultivation of the physical. Work in the fields and around the grounds of monasteries was probably the only activity that kept the monks physically fit. When such work was transferred to the laity and more intellectual pursuits became the rule for them, even this basic physical fitness was lost. As is so often the case, the pendulum had swung too far in the other direction.

the age of chivalry

Physical education was revived to a degree in the Age of Chivalry. Feudal society was divided into three classes: 1) the masses, who had to work very hard to support the other classes and eke out a bare subsistence for themselves; 2) the clergy, who carried on the affairs of the Church; and 3) the nobles, who were responsible for the government of certain lands or territories under a king, and who performed the necessary military duties. In this period a physical and military education of the most strenuous type was required of the knight along with prescribed training in social conduct to enable him to serve his feudal lord, the Church, and all women. Such an ideal was undoubtedly better in theory than in practice, but it did set higher standards than those which had previously existed. The aim of physical education was certainly narrow, and health standards were usually frighteningly poor by present standards. With the loss of the Greek ideal, physical education once again served a most practical objective—that of producing an individual well trained in the art of hand-to-hand combat, possessing all the necessary physical attributes (*e.g.,* strength, endurance, agility and coordination). With the subsequent invention of machinery of war, the enemy was not always met at close range. As a result, death in battle became to a certain degree accidental and was not necessarily the result of physical weakness. Naturally, some divergence resulted in the aims and methods of military training and those of physical education.

a transitional period

With the decline of feudalism and the rise of an early type of nationalism, trade became more vigorous and towns grew up. A stronger middle class gradually arose with a resultant demand for an improved educational system designed to prepare youth for its lifetime occupations. During this time some physical education of an informal nature contributed to the social life and recreations of the young townspeople, as well as to their military training. Games and sports were accompanying features of frequent religious holidays.

THE RENAISSANCE

The historical period which followed feudalism became eventually known as the Renaissance. It was natural that learned people should begin to look back at the periods in history in which similar societies had existed. The Church was solidly entrenched, and there was much enthusiasm for scholarship in the professions of law, theology, and medicine. The scholasticism of this period, with its emphasis on intellectual discipline, found little if any room for physical education, however. Unorganized sports and games were the only activities of this nature in the cathedral schools and universities. In the late fourteenth and fifteenth centuries, however, a philosophy called humanism developed; scholars rediscovered old Greek and Latin texts which sang the praises of the individual. Thus, once again, after many centuries the physical side of man was not overlooked. Most humanistic educators appreciated the value of the earlier Greek ideal and emphasized the care and proper development of the body. Vittorino da Feltre, at the court of the Prince of Mantua in northern Italy, set an example in physical education methods in his school. His aims were to discipline the body so that hardship might be endured with the least possible hazard; his pupils were some day to bear arms and had to know the art of war. Sports and games of an individual and group nature were included because of the recreative value of such activity. He believed further that the ability of youth to learn in the classroom depended somewhat upon the physical condition of the boy involved.

EARLY MODERN PERIOD

As the schools lost their original aim, concentrating exclusively on the study of the classical languages and neglecting the other aspects of these civilizations, there followed once again a decline in liberal education. The importance of physical education also declined, as preparation for lifework was crowded out of the curriculum by preparation solely for university education. When the spirit of Italian humanistic education finally spread over all Europe, the Greek ideal of physical education had lost strength and was realized only by relatively few individuals. The Protestant Reformation did nothing to encourage physical education activities—with the possible exception of Martin Luther himself, who realized a need for the physical training of youth. Certain educators did rebel against the narrow type of education that had come into vogue, but they were the exception rather than the rule. Rabelais satirized contemporary education by his depiction of the typical Latin grammar school graduate; his Gargantua was a "dolt and blockhead," who subsequently became a worthwhile person when his education became more well-rounded. Michel de Montaigne, the great French essayist of the sixteenth century, believed that the education of man should not be divided into two parts—mind and body. Other educators, such as Locke, Mulcaster, and Comenius, also recognized the value of physical exercise and attainments. In the seventeenth century, character education was the primary aim, but health and physical fitness were stressed as underlying needs. Locke, for example, stressed the importance of recreation for youth, an idea that unfortunately was not accepted as the ideal in a society characterized by a variety of social classes.

FROM THE EIGHTEENTH CENTURY TO THE PRESENT

eighteenth-century Europe

The eighteenth century was a period of change to what would today be called more up-to-date political, social, and educational ideals. In France, Voltaire denounced both the Church and the State. Jean Jacques Rousseau decried existing social and educational patterns; he blamed social inequality and civilization itself for a great deal of the unhappiness in the world. His solution?—a "back to Nature" movement, which would eliminate this degeneration caused by man and his contrived societal groupings. In his famous educational work, *Émile,* he portrayed what he considered the ideal education for a boy. From the age of one to five, the only concern should be for the growth and physical welfare of the child's body. From five to twelve years of age, the idea of natural growth was to be continued as the sturdy, healthy youngster learned something about his environment. Rousseau considered the individual to be an indivisible entity and was firmly convinced that lifelong growth was possible. For him it was difficult to determine when an activity lost its physical value and possessed intellectual worth alone.

The opinions of both Rousseau and Voltaire, combined with other social influences did lead to the ruination of the existing social order and helped to bring about its reconstruction in the next century. For example, Johann Basedow started a naturalistic school in Dessau according to the ideas of Rousseau. This school, called the Philanthropinum, was the first school in modern Europe to admit children from all social classes and give physical education a place in the daily curriculum. A number of other prominent educators expressed themselves relative to the proper place of physical education in the educational curriculum and helped to influence public opinion in the late eighteenth century. Outstanding among these men were GutsMuths, Kant, and Pestalozzi. Friedrich Froebel, who ranks along with Pestalozzi as a founder of modern pedagogy, offered the first planned program of education through the medium of play.

emerging nationalism

Physical education in modern Europe has been very closely connected with emerging nationalism. Both the French and the American Revolutions sparked feelings of national loyalty in many parts of the world. Gradually education has been recognized as a vital means for promoting citizenship and thus, indirectly, economic and political stability. The development of national interest per se appears to have been most useful in bringing about necessary social reform; now, however, as we think more in terms of a world government, we must seek to place greater stress upon the cultural contributions each nation has to make. Physical education and sport typically have been used to promote physical fitness and the desire to excel in competitive sports. Now, however, the cooperative as well as competitive aspects of physical education and sport should be stressed. Let us compare our systems with pride but not strive to "beat our opponents into the ground on the field of friendly strife." Competition in a wide variety of sports among nations can be thrilling, adventurous, and educative. But to overemphasize it to the extent of maintaining that we must win to prove our way of life is best and to introduce the Cold War into sports and athletics, merely defeats our purpose.

Germany

The German gymnastic societies (Turnverein) originated in the first decade of the nineteenth century. Friedrich L. Jahn, a staunch patriot of the time, is considered the father of this movement. He wanted his people to become strong enough to throw off French domination. Jahn believed not only that exercise was a means of growth and development for the individual, but also that there was a certain mental and moral training to be derived from experience at the "Turnplatz." Prussia's War of Liberation (1813) undoubtedly owed its success in some measure to his work. "Turnen" underwent periods of popularity and disfavor during the next forty years, and the Turnverein only reluctantly accepted the games and sports of the modern period.

Adolph Spiess did a great amount of work in planning and developing school gymnastics, as he strove to have physical training included as an important part of the child's education. In 1849 he established normal classes in gymnastics at Darmstadt, and his influence was subsequently felt in the various school systems of Germany. In contrast to Jahn's informal, leisurely approach to gymnastic training, Spiess emphasized its formal aspects. Down through the years there have been efforts to broaden the scope of physical education in keeping with changing educational philosophies and political regimes. The National Socialists, of course, gave a strongly militaristic flavor to physical education and used it as an important means of glorifying the supremacy of the state. Such use of physical education and sport deserves most careful study.

Great Britain

Great Britain's isolated position in relation to the Continent made rigorous training for warfare and national defense somewhat less necessary and tended to foster the continuance of interest in outdoor sports. In feudal England archery was the most popular sport; in the fifteenth century it was rivalled by golf, an activity that was soon banned by law because of the disturbance it created. A little later, however, it became quite popular with the nobles. Field hockey, cricket, bowling, quoits, tennis, rugby, hammer throwing, and pole vaulting had their origins in the British Isles. Many other traditional sports originated elsewhere but were soon adopted by the English people.

In the early nineteenth century, an urgent need for systematized physical training was felt. Clias, Ehrenhoff, Georgii, and Maclaren were some of those who introduced varied methods of physical education to the British people. The new interest in systematic school gymnastics and the movement for improved health do not seem to have interfered with participation in sports, however. Down through the years Great Britain has encouraged active participation by all school children and avoided overtraining the few. This has been evidenced by the stress on team games as a means of socialization and of developing desirable personality traits. Other European systems of physical education have periodically received attention in Great Britain (*e.g.*, Swedish gymnastics), but it can be fairly said that Britons have never neglected the educational aspects of physical education in the twentieth century nor the fundamental principles of exercise to promote health and physical fitness.

Sweden

The development of modern physical education in the Scandinavian countries has been significantly related to the nationalism so evident throughout Europe as a whole. Sweden, like many countries in Northern Europe, underwent periods of conflict, resulting eventually in severe delimitation of its once extensive empire; Russia's conquest of Finland in 1808 left Sweden with approximately two-thirds of its former territory. It is no wonder, therefore, that the Swedes felt a desire to regain their prestige—much in the same way that the Germans did after the victories won by Napoleon.

Per Henrik Ling (1776–1839) is credited as the man who gave the greatest impetus to Swedish physical education. Having studied in Denmark under Nachtegall, he brought his newly-found knowledge and experience back to his homeland. With his characteristic drive and enthusiasm, he secured acceptance of a program of gymnastic activities designed to improve the physical fitness of Sweden's military forces. In addition he saw that properly designed exercise programs could do much to improve the health of the entire populace. Known as "medical gymnastics," this aspect of Ling's total educational program was designed to produce a well-balanced organism.

Those who followed Ling temporarily lost sight of his broad aims, but twentieth-century Swedish physical educators have regained the balance that seemed so basic to him—a balance that can be characterized as an essentialistic approach, leading ultimately to both physical and mental health. All types of sports are encouraged, especially those which lend themselves to the climate of this geographical area. Conscious development of character through participation in team sports has received less attention.

France

The French Revolution of 1789 overthrew an absolute monarchy in which the citizens had little or nothing to say about the determination of their own destiny. In each of the thirty-two provinces an Intendant representing the king exercised absolute power. The economy was not stable, and the system of law was not uniform. The actual crisis of the Revolution was preceded by loss of territory in 1763 and many poor administrative decisions by a weak Louis xvi. Such social reformers as Montesquieu, Voltaire, and Rousseau (not, like the others, known as a rationalist) helped to establish the intellectual climate for a rebellion.

With the Revolution came the establishment of the First French Republic. Austria and Prussia, themselves monarchies, attempted to restore the King's ever-weakening power. But the momentum of the Revolution proved too great; after the execution of Louis xvi and Marie Antoinette, a coalition of adjoining powers attempted to conquer France. It was then that Napoleon Bonaparte (1769–1821) came into power. His successes in battle strengthened a weakened French national pride. Through centralized governmental administration he was able to give the situation stability. He improved the system of French law and developed an educational system that extended from the elementary school through the University of Paris. Further struggles lay ahead, however, and for a time it appeared that the French would defeat all of their adversaries. After a truly disastrous Russian campaign, a defeat at Leipzig in 1813, and a subsequent loss in battle at Waterloo, Napoleon was banished. At Vienna in the years 1814–15 the map of Europe was redrawn by the diplomatic representatives of England, Prussia, Russia, Austria, and other less important states.

French physical education development during these years was the result of the work of such foreigners as Francisco Amoros and Phokion Clias. The program was formal in nature and was designed to produce strong, active bodies for the military units. Later on, after the Revolution of 1848, the status of physical training declined until France suffered further loss of prestige in the Franco-Prussian War. At this point efforts were made to introduce sports and games into the lives of youth in order to develop the requisite qualities for a strong and vigorous citizenry. Such names as de

Coubertin, Hébert, Demeny, and Simon are today recognized for vigorous leadership in the early part of the twentieth century.[3]

olympic games revival

At the end of the nineteenth century, Baron Pierre de Coubertin of France brought about the revival of the Olympic Games (1896). Despite the fact that two world wars, and many lesser wars, have been fought since the advent of the modern Olympic Games, the world looks forward with great interest and a feeling of international good will to these Games every four years. The public and the various communications media have persisted in keeping unofficial team scores, although performance is on an individual basis. As a result, winning records in recent years have had definite political overtones for the two camps in the Cold War. Yet there is no doubt that sports and games for both men and women have become increasingly popular in most of the countries of the world, and a certain amount of improved international understanding has resulted from sports competition.

the United States

Finally let us consider the role that physical, health, and recreation education has played in the educational pattern of the United States, since this is of immediate importance to us, and how physical education activities have adapted themselves to changing economic, political, and social conditions.

As the population of colonial America was mostly rural, organized gymnastics and athletics found no place in the daily lives of people. Most of the colonists, with the exception of the group known as the Puritans, engaged in the games and recreational activities of their motherlands as time permitted. The significance of play and its possibilities as an important phase of the educational process were not comprehended; in fact, those who determine educational policies were opposed to the idea of physical education and sport.

The national history of the United States is mirrored, to a degree, in the history of the academies. These schools aimed to prepare youth to meet the many challenges of life, an emphasis that naturally upgraded the position of physical education in the curriculum. Some of the early academies, such as Dummer, Andover, Exeter, and Leicester, were founded and incorporated before 1790. This movement reached its height around 1830 when there were approximately 800 such schools throughout the country.

EARLY SUPPORT. Many of the early American educators and statesmen advocated the idea that both the body and the mind needed attention in our educational system. Captain Alden Partridge, one of the early superintendents of the United States Military Academy at West Point, crusaded for

---

[3] A comprehensive history of physical education would include discussions of the aims of physical education in many other countries throughout the world. Only a few representative countries of the Western world have been discussed in this volume.

the reform of institutions of higher education. He deplored the entire neglect of physical training. Other crusaders included Benjamin Franklin, Noah Webster, Thomas Jefferson, Horace Mann, and Henry Barnard. Through the influx of such men as Charles Beck, Charles Follen, and Francis Lieber, German gymnastics came to the United States in the early nineteenth century. At this time, however, the people did not appreciate fully the value of these activities.

The Turnverein influence made important contributions to physical training shortly before the Civil War. The Turners advocated that mental and physical education should proceed hand in hand in the public schools. The greatly increased enrollment of the elementary and high schools soon made them the outstanding agency for the improvement of national health and physical welfare. Turners were leaders in the physical education movement around 1850 in the cities of Boston, St. Louis, Rochester, and Cincinnati. Two other contemporary leaders were George Barker Winship and Diocletian Lewis. Winship was an advocate of heavy gymnastics and did much to convey the notion that strength and health were completely synonymous. Lewis, who began the first teacher-training program in physical education in the country, a crusader in every sense of the word, desired to improve the health of Americans through a system of light calisthenics. He believed his system would develop grace, flexibility, and agility as well. His stirring addresses to many professional and lay groups did much to popularize gymnastics and to convey the idea that such exercise was more for the weak than for the strong.

POST-CIVIL WAR PERIOD.   After the Civil War, the Turnvereins continued to stress the role of physical education in the educational system. Influencing hundreds of thousands of people through direct or indirect contact, they have always opposed purely military training as a substitute for physical education. In addition, the modern playground movement found the Turners among its strongest supporters. The Civil War had clearly shown the need for a concerted effort in the areas of health, physical education, and athletics. The Morrill Act of 1862 laid the foundation for the establishment of the land-grant colleges. Because of the stress on military drill, however, physical education did not gain acceptance at this time. An extremely differentiated pattern of physical education existed in the post-Civil War era.

American sports, as we now know them, originated in this period of internal conflict. Baseball and tennis became popular in that order. Golf, bowling, swimming, basketball, and a multitude of other so-called minor sports made their appearance in the latter half of the nineteenth century. American football started its rise to popularity during this period. The Amateur Athletic Union, organized in 1888, gave invaluable service toward the promotion of legitimate amateur sport.

The Young Men's Christian Association, which traces its origins back to 1844 in London, when George Williams organized the first religious group, has as its underlying theme that physical welfare and recreation significantly aid moral welfare. Some of the early outstanding leaders in physical education in this organization were Robert J. Roberts, Luther Halsey Gulick, and James Huff McCurdy.

EARLY COLLEGE AND UNIVERSITY PROGRAMS. It was at this time also that many colleges and universities initiated programs which indicated the concern of administrators and teachers about the health of their students. The University of Virginia was the first to have a real gymnasium, and Amherst College followed in 1860 with a two-story structure devoted to physical training. President Stearns urged the governing body to start a department of physical culture whose primary aim was to foster sound health practices. Dr. Edward Hitchcock headed this department for a period of fifty years until his death in 1911. Yale and Harvard erected similar buildings, but their physical training programs did not receive adequate support until somewhat later. Dr. Dudley Allen Sargent, who took charge of Harvard's Hemenway Gymnasium, led his university to a preeminent position in the field of physical education. His program, later adopted by many Midwestern colleges, stressed physical education for the individual and the attainment of a perfect structure (harmony in a well-balanced development of mind and body). From the outset, colleges took the position that games and sports were not necessarily a part of the educational program. Interest was so intense, however, that the wishes of the students could not be denied. They were anxious to demonstrate their abilities in the various sports against young men from other institutions; thus from 1850 to 1880 the rise of interest in intercollegiate sports was phenomenal. Rowing, baseball, track and field, football, and later basketball, were the major sports. The colleges soon found that these athletic sports needed control, as evils began to creep in and destroy the values originally associated with the games.

AN IMPORTANT DECADE. The years from 1880 to 1890 undoubtedly formed one of the most important decades in the history of physical education in America. The colleges, the Christian Associations (Y.M.C.A. and Y.W.C.A.), the Turners, and the proponents of the various systems of gymnastics, all made noteworthy contributions during this decade. The Association for the Advancement of Physical Education was founded in 1885, with the word "American" not being added until the following year. This professional organization was the first of its kind in the field, and it stimulated improved teacher education. The next step for the young field was the promulgation of a planned, organized program of physical education—a program the aims and objectives of which were in accord with the existing educational pattern. Then began the long, slow struggle to bring about the widespread adoption of such a program. Early state legislation for physical education did result before the turn of the twentieth century.

During the late nineteenth century efforts developed in the area of organized recreation and camping for children in underdeveloped areas in the larger cities. The first playground was started in Boston in 1885, followed closely by similar developments in New York and Chicago, as the ill effects of the Industrial Revolution began to be felt. This was the meager origin of the present burgeoning recreation movement in our country. Private and organizational camping got its start before the turn of the century as well and has flourished similarly since that time.

EARLY TWENTIETH CENTURY. In the early twentieth century, Americans showed renewed enthusiasm for discussing the question of educational aims and values. Early American education had been religious in nature but gradually became secularized by an emerging nationalism. As America came into its own economically speaking, educational aims veered from the purely political to the economic. The tremendous increase in high school enrollment forced a reconsideration of these aims at all levels of the system, and the application of scientific methods facilitated this task. In particular, social scientists attempted to state our aims in the light of sociological implications. For the first time, education was conceived in terms of preparing the individual for his role as a citizen of an evolving democracy. John Dewey's writings encouraged the viewing of the curriculum as child-centered rather than subject matter-centered. The Progressive Education Movement, an outgrowth of his thought, placed great emphasis on individualistic aims but countered them by a demand for social rather than purely individual welfare.

The relationship between health and physical education and our educational system developed rapidly during the first quarter of the twentieth century. Health education in all its aspects was viewed seriously, especially after the implications of the draft statistics of World War I were fully comprehended. Many states passed legislation regarding the teaching of physical education in the schools. National interest in sports and games grew at a phenomenal rate in an era when economic prosperity prevailed. The basis for school and community recreation was well laid.

THE NATURAL MOVEMENT. As physical education began to achieve maturity through its introduction by law into a great many schools, the struggle between the inflexibility of the various foreign systems of gymnastics and the individualistic freedom of the so-called natural movement was being waged with increasing vigor. The rising interest in sports and games made the conflict quite unequal, especially after the concept "athletics for all" began to take hold in the second and third decades of the century. The natural movement was undoubtedly strengthened by findings of certain natural and social scientists and thinkers, particularly John Dewey, and the newer method appeared to be more effective in the light of the changing ideals of an evolving democracy. It is certainly also true that the influence of idealism remained strong with its emphasis on the development of individual personality and the possible inculcation of moral and spiritual values through the transfer of training theory applied to sports and games.

SCHOOL HEALTH EDUCATION. Health education likewise made rapid progress during this period. The scope of school hygiene increased, and the importance of the medical examination grew. School health education was gradually recognized as including three major divisions: health services, health instruction, and healthful school living. The need to develop and expand in this area was seen by many, and during this period the tendency began toward some separation between health and physical education. Many physical educators began to be concerned with other aims and were also devoting a great amount of time to athletic coaching duties. The expansion of direct and indirect health education of the general populace through the medium of many private and public agencies tended to draw those more directly interested in the aims of health education away from physical education and athletics.

THE RECREATION MOVEMENT. Progress in the recreation field was most significant as well. The Playground Association of America, organized in 1906, was one response to the recreational need. At this time, however, there was still an extremely close relationship between physical education and recreation because of the keen interest in the aims of recreation by a number of outstanding physical educators. Many municipal recreation centers were constructed, and some of the schools served as after-hour recreation centers. People began to see that recreational activities of all types served an important purpose in a society undergoing basic changes. Some recreation programs developed under boards of education; others involved joint sponsorship of school boards and municipal governments; and a large number of communities placed recreation under the direct control of the municipal government. In the last case, school facilities were rented when possible, or municipalities gradually developed recreational facilities of their own.

1930 TO 1960. Lacking true historical perspective, one finds it extremely difficult to assess the period from 1930 to 1960. The depression of the 1930s, World War II and its aftermath, the Korean conflict, the cold war in general, and now the struggle in Vietnam have been such strong social influences that the development of aims in physical, health, and recreation education seem to have been dominated almost completely by them. It would be elementary to say that school health educators feel more and better health education would be most valuable to students; that physical educators want more and better physical education and intramural athletic programs; and many physical educators and/or coaches are largely involved with efforts to develop outstanding competitive athletic teams and are probably "spreading themselves too thin"; and that recreators see their area of concern becoming more vital to the future of our society and are making every effort to truly professionalize themselves. Yet this is probably an accurate, thumbnail description of the present state of affairs. The energetic American Association for Health, Physical Education, and Recreation, a department of the National Education Association, has accomplished a great deal through the efforts of its approximately fifty thousand professional members. The profession has struggled valiantly to coordinate its various allied movements within the framework of public education and seems to have made real progress. Of course, in light of conflicting educational philosophies, it is no simple matter to determine what is educational—and this is where much of the difficulty lies.

We have seen teacher preparation strengthened through the media of national conferences, accreditation, and self-evaluation. The dance movement has been a significant development. A great deal of progress has been made in physical education research, especially in the physiological area of physical fitness. Furthermore, it has been possible to separate the concepts of physical education and military fitness in many people's minds. The national interest in sport and competitive athletics has continued unabated—indeed has actually grown! Finally, the recent demand for physical fitness improvement in our youth has achieved results primarily because of the dedication of members of the profession and the support received from two Presidents. That there is evidence for encouragement on our part is self-evident, but the value struggle within the field will only intensify unless we can bring about greater consensus. Such understanding will only come through a deeper study and application of scientific and philosophical methods. Since the professional educator has a key role, he needs to be more fully informed in this regard.

In summarizing this first and perhaps most important persistent problem—values (or aims) in physical, health, and recreation education—we should reiterate that the historical aims have been dealt with at some length in order to provide a fundamental background for other persistent problems that will follow. In general educational philosophy we have found *two major viewpoints* on educational values: they are either *subjective* or *objective*. The *progressivist* views educational aims as relative and experimental in a changing world. Specific educational objectives emerge as life goes on, and we learn from experience. The *essentialist,* conversely, looks upon educational values as objective and intrinsic in the universe. They are there because that's the way things are in this world. Consequently, on the essentialist's scale of values intrinsic values take precedence over any possibly instrumental values. The fulfillment of man's inherent potentialities overrides any and all other subsidiary educational objectives.

WHERE DO WE GO FROM HERE? First, we may not even be able to accept the name "physical, health, and recreation education" no matter how the various elements are juxtaposed. The progressivist would readily accept such a name, but the essentialist might be satisfied with just "physical education," or perhaps even "physical training." Determining if he believes that educational values are subjective or objective, experimental or intrinsic helps the individual decide whether he is naturalistic or spiritualistic in his basic outlook. He can now locate his approximate position on the educational philosophy spectrum.

A more difficult problem is examining the major philosophical tendencies in the light of their possible implications for education, as well as for physical, health, and recreation education. Unrefined or naïve naturalism (Rousseau) can probably be eliminated from present-day consideration, because it is now generally considered the pervasive and underlying influence in both experimentalism (pragmatic naturalism) and naturalistic realism. The point of divergence here is the *subjectivity* of values for the pragmatic naturalist and the objectivity of values for the naturalistic realist. After having examined the accompanying diagram and having reread Appendices A and B, you should be able to locate your position a bit more exactly on the spectrum. You may find yourself on the right or the left generally. Still further, you may find yourself to be largely an experimentalist, an idealist, or a realist (either naturalistic or spiritualistic). Or you may discover that you are utopian in your experimentalistic, progressivistic beliefs (a reconstructionist!), or perhaps that existentialism appeals to you most.

THREE MAJOR PHILOSOPHIES

As a result of the foregoing examination, we are now in a position to state that there appear to be *three leading philosophical positions regarding physical, health, and recreation education.* There are, of course, those who say that

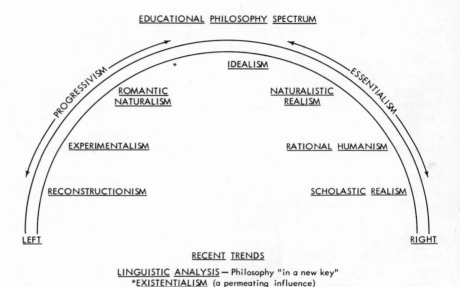

EDUCATIONAL PHILOSOPHY SPECTRUM

PROGRESSIVISM

IDEALISM

ROMANTIC NATURALISM

NATURALISTIC REALISM

ESSENTIALISM

EXPERIMENTALISM

RATIONAL HUMANISM

RECONSTRUCTIONISM

SCHOLASTIC REALISM

LEFT

RIGHT

RECENT TRENDS

LINGUISTIC ANALYSIS — Philosophy "in a new key"
*EXISTENTIALISM (a permeating influence)

the field has no place whatsoever in education, but they are extremists and decidedly in the minority, or perhaps they simply have not worked out their own educational positions consistently and logically. One last thought—these positions are delineated specifically with our way of life in mind.

experimentalism

The first of these three philosophies is *experimentalism* (or *pragmatic naturalism*). The experimentalist is much more interested in promoting the concept of total fitness rather than physical fitness alone. He challenges the name "physical" education. He believes that what is presently called physical education can become an integral subject in the curriculum according to his definition of educational values. Students should have the opportunity to choose useful activities, and there should be a wide selection. Of these activities, many should be of the "socializing" type, since they help to develop what Dewey called "social intelligence." Furthermore, the activities offered should bring natural impulses into play.

The experimentalist believes that the term "evaluation" should be used rather than "tests and measurements," because the former term implies concern with the individual and his progress in relation to his environmental adjustment. He believes further that the concepts of "grades" and academic credit should be replaced by evaluation of student growth in keeping with the competencies and knowledges he has acquired. To him, physical education classes and intramural athletics are more important to the large majority of students than interscholastic or intercollegiate athletics and deserve priority if conflict arises over budgetary allotment, staff availability, and use of facilities. The experimentalist can give full support to team experiences in competitive sports, because they can be vital educational experiences—especially if the elements of competition and cooperation are rather evenly balanced. Furthermore, athletic and recreational activities at a relatively high level of skill can be an aesthetic experience of a fine type. The planned occurrence of educational situations within sports and athletics is also important to the experimentalist. If stress is placed on the continuous development of standards of conduct, such situations can contribute significantly to moral training. Rigorous physical activity for both sexes is desirable and necessary to produce strong, well-poised bodies. Lastly the experimentalist wants to see the three branches of the field more closely coordinated so that experimental aims may be more fully realized.

SCHOOL HEALTH EDUCATION. In the area of health education, the experimentalist views health instruction and first-class health services as vital to every school system. Since health is a primary objective of education for him, the concept of healthful school living should be made a reality at all levels of education. He believes further that natural types of exercise promote sound mental health. As he sees it, the school health education program depends upon the degree of cooperation among home, school, and community agencies. To be truly effective, school health education should be concerned with helping the individual to lead a rich, full life.

RECREATION EDUCATION. The experimentalist believes that education for leisure is basic to the curriculum of the school. For him, overly organized sport competition is not true recreation; instead, play should be conducted in such a way that desirable moral growth occurs. If the proper foundation is laid in the educational system, men will have the opportunity to use their leisure creatively and fruitfully to insure desirable individual growth.

RECONSTRUCTIONIST. A utopian experimentalist, the reconstructionist should be considered briefly at this point. Basically speaking, he would endorse much of what has been said under experimentalism, although he would advocate even more forcefully the individual's self-realization as a social being. The introduction of dance and art into physical education as stimulants of man's creative expression is one project of interest to him. Intramural sports and voluntary recreational activities should be accorded a high place, and this would apply especially to team competition with particular stress on cooperation as a strong element along with the promotion of friendly rivalry. Extramural sport competition could be introduced where the need arises— in other words, striving for excellence is important, but more important is keeping materialistic influence out of educational programs. In the area of health education, many aims of the experimentalist would be duplicated. Two important additions are courses in sex education and family relations, and in mental hygiene. For the reconstructionist would provide a unified program, available on a year-round basis. Relaxation techniques should have a place, as should the whole concept of leisure education, because of the tensions of modern society. School facilities should be accessible for both curricular and extra-curricular programs.

realism

The second of the three major philosophical positions is realism (under which heading may be grouped *naturalistic realism, rational humanism,* and *scholastic,* or moderate, *realism*). Broadly speaking, the realist accepts education "of the physical" as the primary goal. The name of "physical education" by which the field is now generally known doesn't upset him at all. He is concerned with the "development of the maximum of physical vigor," even to the exclusion of the recreational aspects of physical education. Some educational realists recommend that all students in public schools should have a daily period designed to strengthen their muscles, develop their bodily coordination, and improve their cardiovascular endurance. According to the statement of the Educational Policies Commission in 1961, "an adequate physical basis for intellectual life must be assured."

Realists believe that the intrinsic values are more important than the instrumental ones; hence, physical education, even though it is important, must "yield precedence to intellectual education" (however, some naturalistic realists disagree). Most realists give at least qualified approval to interscholastic athletics, as they agree that the learning of sportsmanship and desirable social conduct is important. A leading scholastic realist stated that "sports is a school for loyalty, courage, endurance, determination, universal brotherhood. . . ." Another leading educational philosopher, who calls himself a classical realist, believes that, in the course of his schooling, every child should be required to learn one team game and two individual sports that can be played as an adult, but that such a requirement should be purely extracurricular.

SCHOOL HEALTH EDUCATION. For the realist, health education has an instrumental value; however, those inside the specialized area of physical, health, and recreation education seem to give health instruction and the development of health habits through the medium of the school a more important role. One realist believes that the home must have the complete responsibility for helping youth acquire desirable health habits. He makes an interesting point that "the health of adolescents is for the most part too good and their sources of energy are too great to make health problems real to them." Although he states that sex education is certainly not a proper function of the school, he does advocate fostering the concept of healthful school living, and he suggests further that basic health knowledges do properly belong in the science curriculum. There does appear to be general agreement that a program of physical education should be "based on authenticated health knowledge" and that physical fitness is an important key to a healthy body. The scholastic realist believes that health is decidedly important, but that "the primacy in the human composition does not belong to the body taken from the earth's slime, but to the spirit, to the spiritual soul."

PLAY AND RECREATION. There is a sharp contrast between the realist and the experimentalist when it comes to the question of the role of play and recreation. The realist typically believes that work and play cannot be identified under the same psychological rubric. As one leading educational philosopher explains it, "Play is all right on the playground at recess and after school, but it should not be imported into the regular curriculum." The belief seems to be that adults should think of play as "carefree activity performed for its own sake." With such an approach, the feeling is that recreation can contribute to self-integration through the reduction of psychic tension caused by so many of life's typical stresses. Some educational realists are concerned because the "play attitude" seems to be missing almost completely from organized athletics, and thus, unfortunately, what might be sport—or fun—is kept from being a truly recreational activity. Americans seem to have developed an ambivalent attitude toward play; in other words, if we can make our play serious business, then it cannot be implied or said that we are wasting our time in "sinful" or frivolous activities.

The realist would tend to argue that general education itself is education for leisure, and he would probably concur in the belief that people can develop a number of potentialities for wholesome hobbies through recreation. A leading realistic philosopher of the twentieth century distinguishes relaxation from recreation: "pure relaxation is a necessary condition of health"... "the normal recreation should be change of activity, satisfying the cravings of instincts." In summary, the more essentialistic one's educational philosophy is, the more he sees a sharp distinction between work and play. Although leisure activities of a purely individual benefit do have a place, "winning the cold war" is going to take a lot more hard work and somewhat less leisure.

idealism

Although idealism is considered basically an essentialistic position because of its underlying value theory, its emphasis on the individual and his personality development impinges at certain points on the progressivist side of the educational philosophy spectrum. The idealist believes in education "of the physical," and yet he believes in education "through the physical" as well. Like the realist, however, he sees physical education as necessarily occupying "a lower rung on the educational ladder."

Idealists strive to see man as an organic entity, yet cannot avoid expounding upon the various aspects of man's nature. A leading American physical educator wrote around the turn of the century that "man is capable of development physically, aesthetically, intellectually, socially, politically, religiously, and morally. A man who neglects one or more of these natures is one-sided." He went on to say that developing each of these "natures" to maximum potential was the way to approach life's main goal. A contemporary American physical education philosopher, while subscribing to the idealistic educational hierarchy of values, refuses to underestimate the task of physical education. He reminds us of the status accorded it in Greek idealism and of the new worth it assumes under the transfer of training theory. This psychological theory implies that attitudes of sportsmanship and fair play learned through desirable athletic competition can and do transfer to life situations.

In America, idealism is often associated with the Christian faith. The Young Men's Christian Association, a worldwide movement, has for many years applied Christian ideals to its work in physical education. In 1959, the YMCA listed its five objectives for physical education as follows: 1) development of health and physical fitness; 2) education for leisure; 3) personality adjustment (learning to live with self and others); 4) development of responsible citizenship and group participation; and 5) development of a philosophy of life based on Christian ideals. The last of the above objectives could have well been placed first, for as an outstanding YMCA international leader, Paul Limbert, has stated: "The central emphasis of Christian faith is not on development of the individual as such but on *equipment for service,* both to God and man."

Despite the support that idealism gives to physical education activities, some leaders are concerned about overemphasis, especially in the area of competitive athletics. Limbert warns that "focus on the development of physical strength or athletic prowess runs the risk of self-centeredness," and that sports participation may become an end rather than a means (1961, p. 9). It is feared by another leader that "growing specialization" in sport "tends to reduce the interest of people who are concerned for the whole personality of the participant." Recently established organizations like the Fellowship of Christian Athletes believe that a coach should hold high moral and ethical standards and should set a fine example for his athletes. They would agree with the 1951 position (p. 18) of the Educational Policies Commission that "the basic moral and spiritual value in American life is the supreme importance of the individual personality," and that "the teacher of sports is usually one of the most influential members of the school community in the shaping of moral and spiritual values." A recent educational survey conducted by Wilton (1956, p. 278) reported that a group of seventeen leading American physical educators ratify the idealistic thesis that "creative experience, noble achievement, true friendship, and spiritual satisfaction are encouraged by physical education." Thus, idealism, as seen by one of physical education's spokesmen, believes in "giving the game back to the boys." Character development is paramount; winning scores are incidental in the final analysis.

SCHOOL HEALTH EDUCATION. In the area of health education, we find that the idealist recognizes the importance of sound health in the development of the individual personality, but that it remains "at the bottom of the hierarchy" even though it is "esteemed highly as a basic value for all the others, enhancing the richness of each and all of them" (Horne, *41st Year-*

book, Part I, 1942, p. 186). In an assessment of philosophical values, Clark (now Oestreicher) asserted that idealism stresses "building wholeness of mind and body, ... the development of strong, healthy bodies, ... good habits of mental and physical health, ... and the right start in the teaching of health, safety, and physical education to children" (1943, pp. 310–11). Idealists are concerned as well with the teaching of health knowledges including "attention to sex characteristics and habits, leading to the greater understanding of the place of sex in human life," and the development of proper health habits for sound mental and physical health. In assessing Plato's thought on the subject, Cahn explained that the early idealist saw health as a " 'dynamic equilibrium' between all inner and outer forces with the object of having an individual at harmony with himself and society" (1941, p. 289).

RECREATION AND PLAY. The importance of recreation and play in an idealistic philosophy of education has seemingly not been fully understood or appreciated in the past, and the contributions that this area makes in the education of man should be the subject of scientific research in the light of future needs of our society. The self-expression theory of play appears to be quite compatible with idealism; that is, to the extent that the idealist can realize the eternal values through the choice of the right kinds of play and recreation, he should be progressive enough to disregard a dualistic theory of work and play.

This is not a new idea, but it has been largely disregarded by Christian educators until very recently. Plato, the first idealist, saw the value of play and recreation. He said that "the characters of future citizens are formed through their childhood games," and "play must be, therefore, most carefully utilized and supervised by the state" (Cahn, pp. 289–94). He believed further that "recreation, the activity of leisure, is a necessary alternate with toil to balance the daily life to permit the growth of the integrated man within society." Following this line of reasoning, an idealistic teacher of physical, health, and recreation education would, therefore, be challenged to use recreation and play to combat a deep-seated psychic disintegration that seems to be taking place in a society dominated by materialism. In this way, creative recreation could take on spiritual significance and could relate man to all that is beautiful in life.

OTHER TWENTIETH-CENTURY DEVELOPMENTS

In bringing this particular chapter to a close, it was decided that some assessment ought to be made of current trends in philosophy. A certain amount of communication is now taking place among those who might be designated as philosophers, those who call themselves educational philosophers, and those who, for the first time, are beginning to call themselves physical education philosophers—or who at least say that they are concerned with philosophy *of* physical education, or with philosophy *and* physical education.

In this century it is apparent that there have been strong attacks on many of the traditional approaches. Prior to World War I the idealism that had emanated from Kant had lost some of the prestige it enjoyed in the late 1800s. The defense of scientific investigation by Spencer and Darwin was a tremendously powerful influence. Pragmatism, under the formative influence of a number of early English and European scientists and philosophers and the American triumvirate of Peirce, James, and Dewey, gathered much strength from naturalism and from the continued rise of scientific inquiry. Great emphasis was placed on the desirability of testing hypotheses through experience in order to gain "true" knowledge. In fact, it was stated that we couldn't even know the meaning of an idea before it was put into practice. In educational philosophy, the pragmatic approach is currently known as experimentalism, or pragmatic naturalism.

philosophical analysis

Philosophical analysis emerged as a legitimate philosophical school during the past forty to fifty years. Although various citizens of the Western world have engaged in philosophical thought for more than 2000 years, there is still an argument over the exact nature of the task. Since philosophy seems in some areas, *e.g.*, metaphysics, destined to be superseded by science, many present-day philosophers are concerned about the exact nature of their role. They have apparently concluded that philosophical activity doesn't result in knowledge after all—at least not *new* knowledge. In this century three movements within philosophy have sought to answer this question: 1) logical atomism, 2) logical positivism, and 3) ordinary language philosophy. The main idea behind these approaches is that philosophy's function is analysis— and ultimately, language analysis—but the difficulty is that each posits a different method.

LANGUAGE ANALYSIS. How can language analysis help us in physical, health, and recreation education? This approach may enable the physical education philosopher to clarify the meaning of certain terms, which have been used synonymously for years (albeit often incorrectly); for example, a more careful definition of the terms "sport" and "athletics." Professor James W. Keating of DePaul University in his article, "Sportsmanship as a Moral Category," explains that we have been using the term sport and athletics interchangeably, and therefore loosely and incorrectly (1964, pp. 25–35). Keating explains the difference between the two as follows:

> In essence, sport is a kind of diversion which has for its direct and immediate end fun, pleasure, and delight and which is dominated by a spirit of moderation and generosity. Athletics, on the other hand, is essentially a competitive activity, which has for its end victory in the contest and which is characterized by a spirit of dedication, sacrifice, and intensity. (p. 28)

As Keating adds, we have quite obviously run into a great deal of difficulty by making a "futile attempt to outline a single code of behavior equally applicable to radically diverse activities." By clearly defining our terms, therefore, we can formulate better programs designed to make sound recreative use of leisure time. A careful analysis would in all probability indicate that the field of physical, health, and recreation education is "honeycombed" with ambiguous terminology.

existentialism

During the past 100 years still another philosophy, or at least approach to philosophy, has emerged as a significant force—*existentialism*. Prior to 1850 Sören Kierkegaard had become concerned about the many influences within society that were taking man's individuality, indeed humanity, away from him. Since that time many others have felt a similar concern. Originally, existentialism was a revolt against Hegel's idealism, a philosophy stating that ethical and spiritual realities were accessible to man through reason. Kierkegaard decided that religion would be next to useless if man could reason his way back to God. Nietzsche wished to discard Christianity since science had shown that the transcendent ideals of the Church were nonsense. In his opinion, therefore, man's task was to create his own ideals and values. After all, he was responsible only to himself!

The efforts of twentieth-century existentialists to further this tradition have achieved a considerable amount of acceptance. Some beliefs which characterize modern existentialism involve a continuation of Cartesian dualism that split the world in two. We live in a human world; the world of science extends into mathematical space. Man is part and parcel of this human world and may be distinguished from any and all other animals. Still further, it is not possible to understand man completely through the efforts of natural scientists. There appear to be several different *types* of truth, not just that possible through scientific investigation; thus existentialism argues that science will never be able to answer all man's questions and problems. It becomes an approach to philosophy through which man attempts to look at himself objectively in a world in which God may be dead. Man must blend the past, present, and future together so that the world (the human world) assumes meaning and direction. Man must ask himself what it all means and what action he must take. Can he so direct and guide his own existence that responsible social action will result?

What are some possible implications for education from the existentialistic position? The existentialist is aware that the socialization of the child has become equally as important as his intellectual development as a key educational aim in this century. He is concerned, however, because the leading educational theories "see" the young as objects to be somehow transformed into creatures according to their predecessors' designs. Even the experimentalists seem to have failed in their desire to educate a self-determining man. The existentialist wants an educational system that will help a person to become *aware* of himself as a learner. There should be an individual pattern of education for each unique person.

How might an existentialist regard physical, health, and recreation education? He might agree that this field should strive to fulfill a role in the general educational pattern of arts and sciences. He could well accept a goal of total fitness—not just physical fitness—with a balance between activities emphasizing competition and cooperation. Although the concept of "universal man" is paramount, the individual should be given freedom of choice in physical and health education based on self-evaluation of knowledge, skills, and attitudes. The child who is "authentically eccentric" must be made to feel at home in the physical education activities program. Physical educators should devise opportunities for youth to commit themselves to values and to society. An important problem in sport and athletics is preserving the individual's authenticity in individual, dual, and team sports where winning is so often overemphasized. In sports, as opposed to competitive athletics, a person should be encouraged to select the values he wishes to derive from the activity. Play should be a means to self-actualization—an attempt to use sport for personal purposes. Physical activities in which the opportunity for creativity is important, such as modern dance, should be fully utilized.

What sort of methodology should characterize the existentialistic physical educator's teaching and coaching? The educational process itself should be natural—a give-and-take situation. The student should be allowed to observe and inquire freely. Freedom is most important, but the teacher is needed as the student can't teach himself. A good teacher should show passion, but he should not be egocentric nor too biased about a system or point of view.

Concerning health and recreation education, much of the above material applies. The child must develop an awareness of the need for self-education about the various aspects of personal and community health. Controversial issues should never be avoided. All types of recreational needs and interests should be met through recreation education. One function of play is personal liberation and release. Group recreational activities are good, and have a role, but opportunities for *individual* expression should not be downgraded.

CONCLUDING STATEMENT

This first persistent problem—determining educational values (or aims)—has been treated historically and philosophically at somewhat greater length than most of the other persistent problems included in the text. So that the reader may continue to compare the philosophical stances of the major positions toward other persistent problems, approximately the same procedure will be followed in subsequent chapters.

III

Social Influences

In this chapter four other persistent problems will be discussed at some length. Full historical treatments of these problems, and their various subdivisions, are not presently available. Rather, our task here, and in the following three chapters, is to place each problem in historical perspective before proceeding to a brief philosophical analysis and discussion. These are *our* problems, and it is up to us as a profession to attempt to solve them in the best possible way in our evolving democracy.

THE INFLUENCE OF POLITICS [1]

THREE TYPES OF POLITICAL STATE

The history of the various world civilizations, and their accompanying educational systems, indicates that the kind and amount of education has varied in these societies depending on whether a particular society or country was 1) a monarchy, 2) an aristocratic oligarchy, or 3) a type of democracy or republic.

From the standpoint of sociology, government might be defined as a form of social organization. This organization becomes necessary as a means of social control to regulate the actions of persons and groups. Throughout history every known society seems to have developed some measure of formal control. The group as a whole has been termed the "state," and the members are known as "citizens." Thus, the state is made up of territory, people, and government. If the people eventually unify through common cultural tradition, they are classified as a nation. They develop a pattern of living, called social structure. Political organization is but one phase of this structure, but it exercises a powerful influence upon the other phases. A governmental form is usually a conservative force that is slow to change; inextricably related to the rest of the social structure, the political regime must adapt to changing social organization or anarchy results.

Aristotle's classification of the three types of political states, mentioned above, holds in essence today as it did then. In a society where one man rules, it would seem logical to assume that he should have the best education so that he might rule wisely. The difficulty with this situation is that there is no guarantee that an hereditary ruler is the best equipped person in the entire society to fulfill this purpose.

If the few rule, then they usually received the best education. These people normally rise to power by demonstrating various types of ability. That they are clever cannot be doubted; it is doubtful, however, that the wisest and most ethical people become rulers in an oligarchy.

If the many rule through the power of their votes in democratic elections, it is imperative that the general level of education be raised to the highest degree possible. It becomes part of the ethic of the society to consider the worth of human personality and to give each individual the opportunity to develop his potentialities to the fullest. In return, in order to assure smooth functioning of the democracy, the individual is asked to subjugate his per-

---

[1] It should be understood that the word "politics" is used here in the best sense—the theory and practice of managing public affairs. When we speak of a politician, therefore, the intent is to describe a person interested in politics as a most important profession, and not one who through "shady practices" might attempt to amass personal wealth and influence.

sonal interests to the common good. Harmony between these two antithetical ideals would seem to require a very delicate balance in the years ahead.

WHICH AGENCY SHOULD HAVE CONTROL? Whereas in a totalitarian state there is but one philosophy of education permitted, other types of government allow pluralistic philosophies of education to flourish. Under the latter arrangement the state could conceivably exercise no control of education whatsoever, or it could take a greater or lesser interest in the education of its citizens. When the state does take an interest, the question arises as to whether the state, through its agency the school, the family, or the church shall exert the greatest amount of influence on the child. When the leaders of the church feel very strongly that the central purpose of education is religious, they may decide to take over the education of the child themselves. In a society where there are many different religious affiliations, it is quite possible that the best arrangement is for the church and the state to remain separate.

DEMOCRACY, AN EVOLVING CONCEPT. The implications of this discussion for the professional in physical, health, and recreation education become immediately apparent. It is rather difficult in this instance to define the three major positions as objectively as we seemed to be able to do in the case of the persistent problem of values. It is possible to state that educational progressivism can flourish only in a democratic society, and that essentialism seemingly may exist in either a monarchy, an oligarchy, or a democracy. The key question, of course, is at what point essentialism and the objectives of a democracy conflict. Democracy itself means different things to particular educational philosophers; it is not possible to strike an absolute balance among the conflicting concepts of equalitarianism, freedom, sharing, and respect for man's dignity.

EXPERIMENTALISM NEEDS A DEMOCRATIC SETTING. To refine this line of thinking still further, experimentalism in education would be quickly eliminated in a totalitarian or fascist state. The same would seem to be true for Protestant Christian idealism with its emphasis on cultivation of the individual personality and a higher loyalty to a Divine Being. The essentialistic Catholic Church has often been strong enough to withstand the onslaughts of a strong state which attempts to dominate, but it has been sorely pressed on many occasions.

In our specialized field within education, the experimentalistic belief that physical, health, and recreation education can become an integral experience in the curriculum (according to his definition of educational values) would seem to be realizable *only* in an evolving democracy. The many objectives for physical education emphasizing the concept of "total fitness" can only be projected in a situation where the individual's progress toward these objectives is evaluated in terms of his own starting point. Such an educational climate is also necessary for the achievement of the experimentalist's goal for school health education—an individual capable of "living most and serving best"—and for recreation education.

REALISM FUNCTIONS UNDER VARIOUS TYPES OF STATE. Conversely, the realist can and does function under various governmental regimes. Since physical education is regarded as education "of the physical," it is merely a matter of muscle strengthening and development of cardiovascular efficiency. Physical education yields preference to intellectual education, and sports can be a school for the development of loyalty and courage. In like manner, health is instrumental in achieving the higher purposes in life, and play and recreation are simply means to self-integration through reducing the psychic tension caused by life's stresses. Even here, however, there is the danger that organized sport (athletics of a highly competitive nature) tends to destroy the "play attitude."

POSITION OF IDEALIST NOT AS CLEARCUT

Idealism's position is not as straightforward. Man's physical development can take place in any kind of state, although it must be admitted that physical fitness appears to suffer in a laissez-faire democracy except when war becomes imminent. The development of the other aspects of man's nature (*e.g.,* the idealistic goals of physical education prevalent during Greece's Golden Age) presupposes a society in which the individual and his needs and desires rank high. The intensive and continued participation in sport competition of many in the totalitarian state, or the focus of physical education on the development of strength and other physical attributes for purely militaristic purposes, negates the idealistic concept of the whole personality. The idealistic position in health education would not be jeopardized by the philosophy of state extant, with the possible exception that for some citizens a particular type of political society might not view health as basic and valuable to all aspects of man's personality. The traditional position of idealism since the day of Plato on the importance of play and recreation has been similar to that of the realist. In some types of political society, the need of the individual for a balance between work and play might be slighted. This would disturb the idealist (and the realist as well!). We must also not forget that, for the idealist, the potential of play and recreation for spiritual development has never been fully explored. Thus, the "progressive" idealist would argue that the state should never curb individuality in the matter of creative recreational experience.

POSSIBLE POSITION OF THE EXISTENTIALIST

Initially, let us state that existentialist writers have not turned their attention to the question of the ideal political state. The existentialist would see twentieth-century man as a "homeless creature"; he appears to be seeking new and different kinds of recognition, inasmuch as the so-called earlier stability within society seems to have vanished. Since the existentialist then is basically a seeker, he would feel out of place within a totalitarian regime, which demanded unquestioning obedience and negated the development of individual personality and rights. On the other hand, life in the variety of extant democratic states leaves much to be desired. The problem of an exploding population in so many countries, democratically oriented or otherwise, tends to make man more lonely than ever—even though he may be "rubbing shoulders" with the masses daily. The era of the "organization man" within our democratic, capitalistic society has further destroyed man's identity as an individual. The democratic ideal within a republic does offer him an opportunity to be a vocal, enlightened citizen, but somehow few seem to take advantage of this chance for individual expression that almost guarantees the taker immediate recognition and identity.

Transposed to the educational scene, the existentialist is once again disturbed by the failure of our programs to produce young men and women who show evidence of "self-determining posture." How can we awaken the awareness of the learner so that he will demand a more individualized pattern of education? This should be possible within the pluralistic framework of education in the United States. Specifically, how can we help the child who is "authentically eccentric" to feel at home in our typical physical education program? Insisting that he measure up to physical fitness norms does not appear to be any solution to the problem. Self-evaluation and self-motivation could well be the key to this dilemma, but how can this be realized in large classes where there is insistence upon standardized routines both in physical fitness drills and in sport skills? The existentialist is well aware that we don't yet have the answer to this problem, and he doesn't see much evidence of concern about it either.

physical education under various systems

The implications of state involvement in education concern both progressivist and essentialist. The progressivist, who is concerned with social reform, would favor a democratic state in which the individual could choose his socialistic goals on a trial-and-error basis. The basic question remains, Which agency—the school, the family, or the church—should exert the greatest amount of influence on the child? In a totalitarian state the answer is obvious. When the church decides to educate the child, because it believes the central purposes of education are primarily religious, the role of physical, health, and recreation education tends to decline for both philosophical and economic reasons. In a totalitarian state, the church will be restrained in the achievement of its objectives, but a realistic type of physical, health, and recreation education may flourish. In a society where pluralistic philosophies of physical, health, and recreation education exist, and where the federal government perhaps adopts a laissez-faire attitude, the resultant educational product in our specialized area will tend to be quite uneven. The matter is that simple, and yet that complex!

THE INFLUENCE OF NATIONALISM

some definitions

In the English language the word "nation" is generally used synonymously with country or state, and we think of human beings who are united under a type of governmental rule. These individuals, members of a political community, are usually considered to possess a certain "nationality" within a reasonable period of time. The word "people," having a broader and somewhat ambiguous connotation, normally refers to the inhabitants of several nations or states as an ethnological unit.

The word "nationalism" itself might apply to a feeling, attitude, or consciousness that persons might have as citizens of a nation—citizens who hold a strong attitude about the welfare of their nation, about its status in regard to strength or prosperity. Carlton J. Hayes in *Nationalism: A Religion* (1961) refers to patriotism as "love of country," and nationalism as "a fusion of patriotism with a consciousness of nationality." Nationalism might be defined as a political philosophy in which the good of the nation is supreme. The word is often used incorrectly as a synonym for chauvinism.

HISTORICAL BACKGROUND

Thus defined, nationalism has been evident throughout the history of civilization from the relatively simple organization of the tribe to the complex nation-states of the modern world. Some scholars regard nationalism as a term of relatively recent origin, however, because until the modern period no nations were sufficiently unified to permit the existence of such a feeling. But European heritage reveals many examples of "nationalism." We have only to think of the Greek and Roman cultures with their citizenship ideals and desires to perpetuate their culture. Then, too, the Hebrews believed that they were a people selected by God for a unique role in history, and the Roman Catholic Church developed far-reaching loyalties over a significant period of time.

During the course of medieval history, which flowered into the Renaissance, many rulers and their nobles struggled with the Church for control. Eventually people began to think of themselves as Germans, or Frenchmen, or Englishmen. As some sort of representation on parliamentary bodies became possible for those persons or groups known as the middle class (and in the nineteenth century for the lower class) it is reasonable to assume that they would develop a new type of patriotism, and that this feeling would in time blossom into present-day nationalism.

Nationalism got an early start in England, and the English developed what could be called a truly national life. This more "pure" type of nationalism was brought to America by many of the new settlers, although then and now it has periodically erupted into a concept that might be called irrational. Nationalistic feeling was evident in France even before the Revolution with the development of absolute monarchies and the gradual breaking away from the Church's domination. It has been intimated by some that nationalism is a necessary step along the way to the development of internationalism.

German nationalism was stimulated greatly after the crushing defeat by Napoleon at the Battle of Jena; the German people were forced to take stock of their political organization and to suggest remedies for improvement and subsequent return to power in central Europe. Linking nationalism with the concept of power, however, rather than with freedom has often encouraged a type of chauvinism characterized by dislike and even hatred of other nations and peoples. Such a fusion has occasioned untold hardship and disaster to evolving civilization.

The Industrial Revolution stimulated nationalism through the economic doctrines of mercantilism. And the rejection of free trade did much to hold back the progress of *all* men, both in developed and underdeveloped lands. Men were exhorted to follow a pattern of blind allegiance to a country whose leaders in many cases equated greatness with military power. Thus it was perfectly logical that individual freedom would be subjugated to the "greater glory of the fatherland." Unfortunately, these strongly nationalistic beliefs helped to develop an unreasoning fervor that caused people to accept racist theories blindly—beliefs that have resulted in unbelievable acts by so-called civilized men even in the twentieth century. Thus, balancing the world's hopes for a broader concept of internationalism was this ruthless nationalism, raised to the status of a religion in certain countries of the world. Certainly nationalism, and nationalistic education, has its place in the political spectrum, but every effort must be made to preserve the higher goal of individual freedom.

NATIONALISM IN EDUCATION

Reasoned and controlled nationalism has allowed the educational aims of the Church to coexist with its own, probably because their efforts were in somewhat different spheres. But when nationalism has grown disproportionately, it has swept everything in its path aside. Thus, during wartime the very roots of our democratic republic here in the United States have been visibly shaken by an unreasoned nationalism—necessary, perhaps, under the circumstances but very damaging to our national ideals. Obviously, the more totalitarian a state is, the better nationalism thrives; conversely, it is quite difficult for strong nationalism to develop in a pluralistic state. People living in a democratic society would not be satisfied with a nationalistic education dictated by a minority, but if it were possible for nationalism in education to emanate from the goals of a free people, the common good would then be served. A democracy which is far enough advanced to consider sharing its culture with other countries is well on the way to a concept of internationalism. This stage of advancement, if achieved by the majority of nations, might well prepare the way for the existence of "one world"—an idea regarded as an unrealizable dream by a number of conservatives, but, according to many liberals, the only method of insuring permanent peace.

NATIONALISM IN AMERICAN DEMOCRACY

The influence of nationalism on our field is readily observable. If a strong state is desired, the need for a strong, healthy people is paramount. We need only think of the Medes and the Spartans or, in our own time, Nazi Germany and the U.S.S.R. The situation in the United States, viewed historically, has been discussed by H. J. VanderZwaag (Proceedings of the National College Physical Education Association, 1965). He points out that the United States underwent various stages of nationalism in the nineteenth century—from "national and sectional feelings" to a more firm nationalism after the Civil War, with leanings toward internationalism by the turn of the century. VanderZwaag also indicates that it was quite natural for people to become concerned about an *American* system of physical education as the ties with other cultures were lessening; and this was, in fact, what the resultant merger represented. Then he asks whether nationalism has been the dominant force shaping our physical education policies. His conclusion: physical education has not been cultivated for purely nationalistic purposes; rather, "by 1920, it was evident that the United States had evolved a program of physical education which was characterized by informality and an emphasis upon national sports."

IMPLICATIONS OF EDUCATIONAL PHILOSOPHY FOR PHYSICAL EDUCATION

Experimentalism (and reconstructionism) can flourish only in a democratic society. In our country at present the individual states and the local systems can promote just about any type of program in physical, health, and recreation education for which they can gain support. The Federal Government, through the President's Council on Physical Fitness, is attempting to place what might be called a nationalistic emphasis on the *physical* fitness of youth, but it has absolutely no power to enforce its recommendations unless a specific community desires to proceed along these lines. Even if federal funds are made available to our field under the Elementary and Secondary School Act of 1965, it is still questionable whether communities applying for these funds would feel themselves wholly restricted by governmental regulations. Enforcement of these laws is, of course, complicated by the possibility of various interpretations. Thus, it is almost impossible to promote nationalism in health and physical education when it must emanate from the goals of a free people. If our government should attempt to dictate in this matter, as it has done in actual wartime, the basic educational objectives of our democracy would be threatened.

The realist, conversely, can and does function under various philosophies of state, but the idealist may run into difficulty in a political system where the state begins to encroach on the individual's needs and desires. In a progressive system the state will tend to accentuate the socialistic goals of education. The more totalitarian a state becomes, however, the more control it exercises over the educational system and over each individual in planning for the national welfare.

The existentialist would not be particularly disturbed by the presence of what might be called a "healthy" type of nationalism in a society, but he would be rather violently opposed to the overriding nationalism that destroys individual human aspirations. He would argue that it is up to man to make something out of himself, that he must choose his own values in order to give his life meaning.

The language analyst would approach this problem from a completely different perspective. At the outset he would point out that nationalism is really a very vague concept, and that it is not possible to discuss the influence of a social force on a social institution if we haven't accurately defined what we mean when we use the term "nationalism" today. Some have stated that nationalism is a thing of the past. Others have questioned whether a man must forego all nationalistic tendencies when he becomes an internationalist. What is the difference between a regionalist and a nationalist, or a regionalist and a universalist? What specific forms of nationalism are we seeing at present? If there is only one form of nationalism evident in the United States today, what might *that* form of the phenomenon mean for the conduct of education (and, of course, the conduct of physical, health, and recreation education)? In this way the language analyst would attempt to get at the very root of the problem.

CONCLUDING STATEMENT

Nationalism as a persistent historical problem is still with us and will probably continue to exert an influence on physical education. Even the most advanced states supposedly on their way to internationalism are still exhibiting nationalistic behavior. If nation-states can achieve a relatively stable world order, each one possessing its own "healthy" or creative nationalism, professional physical, health, and recreation educators will not have to worry about the goals of their profession being warped and distorted by overly aggressive nationalists.

section three

THE INFLUENCE OF
ECONOMICS

Broadly interpreted, economics as a field is concerned with what man produces and the formal and informal arrangements that are made concerning the usage of these products. Economists want to know about the consumption of the goods that are produced and who takes part in the actual process of production. They ask where the power lies, whether the goods are used fully, and to what ends a society's resources are brought to bear on the matter at hand.

The long-established social order was greatly disturbed by the advent of the machine age and the factory. Men left their homes and their private enterprises, and in the course of our century women followed them, thereby increasing the disturbance to the societal order. Even the farmer became a businessman and, from simple bargaining at the outset, the complex structure known as the "market" developed. In time transportation became cheaper, and trading areas were consequently greatly enlarged.

With the progress of the machine age, the division of labor was tremendous, and families were often no longer self-sufficient. Industrial organizations mushroomed, and the articulations among these various groups were often disorganized. New inventions and products became part of the evolving culture and in turn created new demands. As a result of all of this, man seems to be seeking stability—or at least a reasonable semblance of order. Such stability is not yet in sight; paradoxically, change has become the only relatively certain factor in life. Such social forces as "creeping automation," small wars and possible large wars, space travel, the exploding body of knowledge in all areas, to name only a few, are continually disturbing the economic organization within, between, and among societies. Other influencing factors within the field of economics itself have been organization in the production of goods, mass production, organized research, and the general organization of business, labor, and consumers.

HISTORICAL BACKGROUND

For thousands of years people lived in small, relatively isolated groups, and their survival depended on their own subsistence economy. Early civilizations had to learn how to create surplus economies before any class within the society could have leisure for formal education or anything else that might be related to "the good life." Athens, for example, did not have a "Golden Age" until it became a relatively large commercial and cosmopolitan center. Although the Romans amassed great wealth and developed an extensive educational system, their education remained basically of instrumental, rather than intrinsic, value to the culture. When the Empire declined politically and economically, educational decay set in as well. Then it was necessary for the Roman emperors to subsidize education from the central treasury.

During the early Middle Ages, education suffered as the economy again become agrarian in nature. Later, with the surge in trade and industry, vocational education was provided for the sons of the middle class merchants. The gradual intellectual awakening and then the rise of a spirit of scientific inquiry during the Renaissance, coupled with more profitable commerce and industry, revived education still further. However, only a very small portion of the population ever had enough wealth to gain the leisure necessary for education and cultural pursuits.

The Industrial Revolution brought about marked social and economic changes; as group after group gained wealth they demanded recognition in government. Gradually the masses, supported by educational theorists, clamored for more educational opportunities, and elementary and secondary education became increasingly available on a variety of bases. Class-structured education remained a problem in many countries of Europe despite the existence of steadily improving economies. It is now possible, but still somewhat difficult, for a boy or girl to rise above the social and/or economic level of the family. However, the truly brilliant young people do have this chance.

The United States has now reached a stage where approximately forty percent of its young people go on to some form of higher education. There are still many obstacles to be overcome, as a portion of the population is still "disenfranchised" because of poor educational and family backgrounds. Our economy has now reached a point, however, where young people are being urged to stay in school to avoid a glutting of the labor market. Very soon compulsory attendance beyond the age of sixteen years may be required in many states. This will be possible only because automation is giving us increasingly the type of surplus economy in which a smaller number of people will have to work fewer hours to provide life's necessities. As increasingly more people achieve a greater amount of leisure, the challenge to education and our specialized field becomes very great indeed.

In summary, therefore, education has prospered when there was a surplus economy and declined when the economic structure weakened. Thus, it may be said that "educational cycles" of rise and decline seem to have coincided with economic cycles. Despite these developments, historically formal education has rarely included programs of study about economics that could be described as significant and thoroughgoing—particularly in general education curricula. Similarly, it has been traditional to regard vocational areas of study with less esteem than the liberal arts or humanities.

Educational aims will tend to vary depending upon how people make their money and create surplus economies. There is not much time for "schooling" in the typical agrarian society, because people have to work long and hard. If commerce is added to the agrarian base in a country, education will advance still further as people will ask more from it to meet the needs of the various classes involved. Modern industrial economy has made still further demands on education and has produced the monies whereby it might be obtained.

THE PROBLEM IN A MODERN SOCIETY

Advancing industrial civilization has brought many advantages, but it has created many problems as well. One of these has to do with specialization in function—some people manage and others labor, and this results in an uneven distribution of wealth. Of course, there has always been specialization of function of one sort or another in societies, and the leaders have invariably seemed to end up with the lion's share of the "good things of life." The labor movement is striving mightily to reverse this result to a reasonable degree (although there is certainly no general consensus as to what the word "reasonable" means in this context). The seemingly inevitable existence of classes has had a definite effect on the educational structure. People with more money have been able to afford longer periods and different types of education for their children. It is not difficult, therefore, to understand why the social welfare state concept has been popular with the middle and lower classes and, incidentally, why the Democratic Party, which has traditionally designated itself as the party of the people, has more registered voters in the United States than its rival. Although this is a great oversimplification, there is undoubtedly enough truth in it to warrant further consideration.

Essentialistic education has tended to preserve the culture of the past—the cultural heritage—and its advocates would not be striving for the same sort of change, and certainly not at the same rate, as progressivists. If it is inevitable that there will always be classes of society sharply divided, and that those who work with their hands will be considered inferior (really a most unfortunate connotation), the only hope for the masses is probably in increased educational advantages made possible through continued technological advancement and automation. Much has been written in the United States about the possibility of a classless society, and certainly many of the advantages of "the good life" are increasingly being made available to all. Some educational philosophers predict the coming of a day when all people will profit from a general education—an education that would enable them to participate more fully as individuals and as members of a democratic society. We in the United States have sought to recognize talent in any person no matter what his socioeconomic status, and to give him the opportunity to realize his potential. One of the unfortunate outcomes of this trend has been that the "cream has been skimmed off" many of our less fortunate communities—the ghettos—and we have developed no means to put it back again.

What does this mean to us in the field of education? It means that we have to make a choice as citizens as to which type of economic society we wish to promote. If we feel that this is a world in which people exhibit "golden, silver, and copper" talents and should be educated accordingly, an uneven distribution of wealth will continue. Such a realistic appraisal and approach will undoubtedly encourage the continuance of educational opportunities to those who are able to pay for it. This has meant traditionally that "cultural education" will rank much higher than mere "job training."

On the other hand, the social progressivist will encourage the development of a type of state which will make its many educational advantages increasingly available to all to the limit of their potential.

IMPLICATIONS FOR PHYSICAL, HEALTH, AND RECREATION EDUCATION

Professionals in physical, health, and recreation education rarely give much consideration to the influence of economics until they begin to feel the pinch of "economy moves" at certain times. Then they find that some segments of the society consider their subject matter area to be less important than others, and the people representing these groups decide that physical education or varsity athletics, for example, should be eliminated, or at least sharply curtailed. Such a move often comes as a distinct shock, and it is frequently rationalized by our claim that athletics is being used as a "lever to pry more funds" from a recalcitrant and pleasure-seeking public who would not wish to see its "spectacles" discontinued.

Physical education, especially as it connotes education of the physical, has a good chance for recognition and improvement under either type of economic system. In largely agrarian societies physical fitness normally results automatically through hard work. An industrial society, on the other hand, must prescribe programs to ensure a minimum level of physical fitness for all, either through manual labor or some other type of recommended physical activity. If the distribution of wealth is markedly uneven, the more prosperous groups might achieve their physical fitness through a variety of means, artificial or natural. In a welfare state, where a person would enjoy a relatively longer period of educational opportunity, society would have to decide to what extent it can or should demand physical fitness of all its citizens and how to achieve its end. Here the major philosophical positions in education would "dictate" value structures; physical education would be accorded a higher or lower rank depending on which educational philosophy prevails.

health education

Health education within the schools, with its subdivisions of health services, health instruction, and healthful school living, has developed tremendously in the United States during the twentieth century, and it is now generally recognized that through the educative process youth will develop wholesome health attitudes, habits, and skills.

The same health problems which arise in a democracy could obviously occur in a country under a different political regime; the more influential factors here are climate, geography, and state of economic development. Health standards, generally speaking, are higher in those countries where scientific investigation is on a higher level and where the attitudes of the people act to create a more healthful environment. Such advancement usually means that more money has been made available for research, for environmental change, and for improved public health and school education programs.

A social welfare state would be more concerned about meeting the health needs of people through democratically approved taxation funds to governmental agencies and to schools and through donations of interested individuals and groups to private agencies dedicated to the improvement of national health. An economy with an uneven distribution of wealth would be inclined to spend a lesser amount on the health of the masses, with the best health care going to those who can best afford it. This is true to a degree even in the United States, although people in the lower income brackets can often get fine medical attention if they have the patience to wait in line at a clinic. It is the ever-expanding middle class which many times is "priced out of the market" unless these persons have the foresight, or are forced, to enroll in one of the many private health insurance plans.

It should be pointed out in passing that the rising tide of nationalism throughout the world in the so-called underprivileged countries will undoubtedly bring about improved health education, since leaders will see to it that the populace is strong and healthy whether or not public opinion is entirely favorable to the necessary expenditure. The developing concept of internationalism through UNESCO and related agencies holds great promise for the improvement of health standards around the world. In addition, since the onset of the cold war, East and West are often found vying with each other to give (or to lend) money for the adoption of health measures in many countries.

recreation education

The first condition for recreation education is leisure, and leisure comes about only in a surplus economy. Secondly, the amount and types of recreation education for school age youth, and for other age groups as well, depend a great deal on the prevailing educational philosophy in an educational system. In the United States some leaders have predicted that automation will force our society to prepare people for improved use of expanding leisure. In a society where uneven distribution of wealth is not curbed, the wealthy will have the most expensive recreational pursuits, while the masses will have less time for play and recreation, even of an educational nature. In such an economic system, past experience has shown that cultural education is rated much higher than vocational education. Granted that the educational realist, and many of the idealists as well, views cultural education *as* education for leisure as well as transmission of the social heritage, this would still mean that the masses would receive less cultural education. Thus, the larger part of the population living in such a society would be deprived of knowledge and skills for recreational enjoyment.

In a state where interest in social welfare is high, however, both cultural and vocational education are accessible to all once a surplus economy is attained. Special features of this system include community recreation and adult education. With increasingly more people enjoying their leisure as they see fit, recreation educators can only hope that the standard of living will continue to rise and that educational and recreational opportunities will meet the challenge. In order to ensure this, economists must be encouraged to devise improved methods of preventing economic cycles and material wealth must not be allowed to spoil us and jade our senses as to what a *high* standard of living might really mean. Finally, scientists must discover substitutes for the natural resources that are being steadily dissipated.

THE INFLUENCE OF RELIGION

Religion may be defined broadly as "the pursuit of whatever a man considers to be most worthy or demanding of his devotion" (J. Paul Williams, 1952, p. 350). To be completely religious, therefore, a man would have to devote himself completely to the attainment of his highest aim in life. The more usual definition of religion explains it as a belief in a Supreme Creator who has imparted a spiritual nature and a soul to man and who may possibly guard and guide his destiny. Because there are so many types of religion in the world, and these are in various stages of development, it is well high impossible to present a definition that would be meaningful and acceptable to all.

FOUR STAGES OF RELIGIOUS DEVELOPMENT

In order to understand the evolution of religious thought, we may trace four stages, consequent to one another: 1) animism, 2) animatism, 3) polytheism, and 4) monarchism (S. G. Champion and D. Short, 1951, pp. 1–5). *Animism* is described as primitive man's realization that there were many natural occurrences in the world over which he had no control. Powerful spirits or beings seemed to cause these catastrophes and hardships. What was he to do in order to stop or to lessen the effects of these unpleasant happenings? The best course of action seemed to be appeasement of these angry spirits which might be in the fire or the wind.

The second, more advanced stage is designated as *animatism*. Man had gained more knowledge about natural phenomena; some of them he learned to control to a certain extent, or at least he was able to make some adaptation which made him less vulnerable to their adverse effects. The idea of nature-spirits in stones and trees lessened, and he began to conceive of greater, less personal influences. Seasonal change came to be regarded as the "work" of a very powerful "God."

There is a division of opinion as to what happened next. Some scholars believe that monotheism was the next stage. This happened when a particular tribe accepted a tribal deity. Subsequently, certain tribes were organized into larger groups, according to this theory, and they compromised by accepting each tribe's god and developed a "Pantheon" including many deities. In this way it is theorized that a third stage known as *polytheism* developed naturally as the gods became increasingly more important and powerful. Of course, it is conceivable that both monotheism and polytheism were occurring but in different periods of time and in tribes far distant from each other.

The fourth stage is generally considered to be *monarchism*. This was an approach in which the high priests (and perhaps subsequently the people) select one god as the greatest of all. The other gods would then tend to become less powerful and important. Since man's own social organization was hierarchical, it was only natural for him to see such a hierarchy among the gods. It followed therefore that this greater god was right much more than the lesser deities. If he were all wise, it stands to reason also that he would tend to be just in his dealings with people. The bad people would eventually be punished, and those who were good would be rewarded.

At some stage in this development people became concerned about where God "lives." Hallowed places (shrines) were constructed which later took the form of churches and temples. Certain groups in particular societies believed further that the various gods needed a place where they could live together—a separate world at some distant point up in the sky.

Eventually it wasn't sufficient for gods merely to visit their temples. So the idea gradually spread that gods could return to earth and thereby become involved with men's many problems. A further refinement of this belief was the concept that it was possible for God to become embodied in human form—the idea of *Divine Incarnation*. Still another method whereby God could establish a most intimate relationship was considered to have taken place. It was called *Immanence*—a situation where God was present somehow within the very structure of the earth and the universe.

In the course of this development from animism to monarchism, people came to believe that God had three aspects: 1) He was eternal, existing endlessly apart from the world he created; 2) He had the power to take the form of a man (incarnation); and 3) He was an omnipresent Spirit dwelling in all things. It now becomes quite understandable how the doctrine of the *Trinity* (Father, Son, and Holy Ghost) grew and was subsequently expressed in the creed of the Christian Church.

Along with man's concept of God came a self-concept, distinguishing him from other creatures. He had something in his makeup that animals didn't have—a soul which was believed to be immortal and separable from the body at death. Although man could not describe it accurately, he felt that this entity was the animating principle of his life.

Now man had a God—one God—who possessed infinite power, holiness, wisdom, and foreknowledge. Here was a concept achieved through tremendous endeavor and struggle, although many men were unwilling to accept it. Upon this concept were founded the major religions of the world; in the West Christianity and Judaism subscribe to this belief, although there is much disagreement among the various branches of both these faiths.

Many persons do not give assent to the more orthodox religious beliefs. *Skepticism* holds that absolute truth and knowledge are not available to man, although partial knowledge may be possible. *Agnosticism* seems to go one step further in positing that knowledge of the ultimate origin of the universe is impossible. Lastly, there is *atheism,* a position in which there is complete disbelief in a God or Supreme Power underlying the cosmos.

We have followed the approach that there have been four stages in man's religious development; however, now a fifth position has emerged which some regard as an extension of the fourth position. Man has looked at reality, which he may call God, and has conceived of some sort of partnership. Some consider God to be a friendly partner, if we work according to his physical laws. Recently many churchmen and religious scholars, as an extension of the "friendly partner" position are postulating the idea of a rather democratic, cooperative God as a foundation for a new world order. Religious liberals find difficulty in accepting this position. While recognizing their debt to Christianity and Judaism, they are uniting on a "free-mind principle" instead of any common creed. Some of this group—those who believe in natural order and evolution and who spell man with a capital "M"—have been designated as naturalistic humanists by themselves and others. The religious liberal then is a free spirit who gives allegiance to the truth as he sees it; he seeks to communicate with all liberals no matter to which of the world's twelve great religions they nominally belong.

Another significant reaction to orthodox religion during the past one hundred years has been existentialism. This philosophy has been discussed under our first persistent problem (see pp. 19f). Here let it suffice to say that, on the religious plane, existentialism stressed man's ultimate dependence on God to reveal himself rather than upon man's finding God through reason. For many, though, God had already ceased to exist; man's task, therefore, was to create his own ideals and values, inasmuch as he was responsible only to himself. Twentieth-century atheistic and agnostic existentialists (and it should be stressed that there are Christian existentialists as well, who view all of this differently), *e.g.*, Sartre, are striving to further the existentialist view of man as a unique historical animal making a valiant attempt to look at himself objectively in a world in which God may be, and probably is, dead.

In the pages above, designed to trace in broad outline man's religious experience, no attempt has been made to indoctrinate the reader. The premise here is that *each and every educator* should work out this problem for himself, inasmuch as his decision will undoubtedly have an influence on his development as an individual and as an educator.

THE INFLUENCE OF RELIGION ON EDUCATION

The Christian contribution to the history of the world, and especially to education, has been enormous. For the first time (in the Western world at any rate) the ideas of a universal God and the brotherhood of man took hold. In addition, the Christian emphasis upon the after-life entailed a strict moral preparation. Actually, the basis for universal education was laid with the promulgation of these Christian principles emphasizing the worth of the individual.

The early Church was concerned with moral reformation. The previous, strongly pagan centuries of the Roman Empire had introduced vices which were most difficult to obliterate. The Christians set up many types of schools to help accomplish this purpose, and for a long period the main concerns of monastic life and education were asceticism, chastity, poverty, and obedience. It wasn't until later that the monastic school became interested in the expansion of knowledge and became more tolerant of inquiry. Scholasticism aimed 1) to develop faith and 2) to discover truth through the method of logical analysis. St. Thomas Aquinas (1225?–1274), like Aristotle, shared the spirit of the realist. After most serious consideration, he stated his belief in the reality of matter as the creation of God. He saw God as the first cause— an Absolute with eternal and infinite qualities.

The Protestant Reformation influenced education greatly, while lessening to a considerable degree the all-powerful position of the Catholic Church. The authority of the Bible was substituted for that of the Church, and individual judgment was to be used in the interpretation of the Scriptures and Christian duty. This outlook required the education of the many for the purposes of reading and interpreting God's word. Thus the groundwork was laid for democratic universal education in place of the education of the few for leadership (*e.g.*, the clericals).

In the United States, as the educational ladder extended upward toward the middle of the nineteenth century, religious education was removed from school curricula because of many conflicts. Catholics felt so strongly about the need for religious instruction for their children that they began their own system of education. Protestantism, however, went along with the secularization of the schools, a great boon for the country but perhaps not for Protestantism in the long run. The home has done reasonably well in the inculcation of morals, but with rising materialism and the seeming decline of the family as an institution certain problems have arisen. Many parents no longer seem qualified, nor do they seem to have the desire, to pass on the Christian tradition. One hour a week of Sunday school instruction does not appear to be doing the job adequately. Protestantism's neglect of religious education may in time threaten its very survival, and some argue that this has occurred simply because of a democratic approach to church government. To be fair, it should be pointed out that many Catholics are concerned about the lasting effects of their system of religious education as well.

The position of Catholic realists must be clarified; they still believe that the Catholic Church has the primary role in the education of children and that secular control *cannot* be the only jurisdictional power in such a basic responsibility. This belief includes the explicit idea that salvation is achieved through God's grace *and* through good works following Christ's example and teaching. The implications for education are straightforward: if there are unchanging educational objectives, man on earth must concern himself with the means necessary to achieve this ultimate union with God. This view of education as preparation means that the child must be prepared for an eventual life of reason, and, obviously, the three R's are basic along with science, literature, geography, history, and perhaps a foreign language. Character training is tremendously important in elementary education and, at the secondary level, every young person should have a greater or lesser amount of general education and preparation for life through the learning of a trade (if he is not going on to a university).

A separate educational system is supported by Catholics at considerable hardship, since they pay taxes for public schools too. Apparently they feel very strongly that the civil government does not have the right to educate the child—in certain areas at least. However, the goal of educating every Catholic in a full-time Catholic school is at present unrealizable. If a Catholic school is available within reasonable distance, parents are encouraged to send their children to it. What is really important, of course, is that the child receive religious instruction from qualified teachers. In a situation where religious orientation is so important, and where it can become a reality so naturally within the atmosphere of a Catholic school, it is understandable that the Catholic would consider moral training not properly dealt with in a public school.

Discussion often arises concerning: 1) which agency shall educate the individual—the home, the church, the state, or some private agency; 2) whether or not any agency is capable of performing the task alone. In a democracy each agency would appear to have a specific function to perform in completing the entire task. In Nazi Germany the state attempted to handle the majority of the responsibility. In the United States the Catholic Church combines with the home to perform this all-important function and has succeeded to a great degree. The experimentalist would certainly not agree with much of Catholic methodology and curriculum content. He would tend to place the major responsibility on the home and the school, whether this school was sponsored by the local community and the state or by some private institution. Many under the progressive banner, notably Protestant Christian idealists, believe that the church has a definite task to fulfill in educating the spiritual nature of man, but the pragmatic experimentalists can visualize this function being carried out successfully by the school alone. In the United States today, however, parents must decide for their own children whether religious values, broadly or "narrowly" conceived, *will* be inculcated, and in what way.

History has shown that public schools have not been hostile to religion as such. Sectarianism during the modern period has made it difficult to teach "the Christian religion" in the public schools. Just after the Second World War, the province of Ontario, Canada, decided to include Protestant religious instruction in its public schools. This should be an interesting development to watch, since it is predicted that by 1980 Catholics will outnumber Protestants. In the United States there has been continuous concern about the inculcation of religious and moral values in the public schools despite the separation of church and state. With at least eleven major religious groups in the world, it does seem that some sort of comparative religious education should be taught. This has happened only rarely, because it is so difficult to find an instructor who would be acceptable to the various factions concerned.

Increasingly, world opinion charges that society in the United States is wholly organized on the basis of materialism, and not religious principle. There appears to be a low level of public morals, much political corruption, many dishonest businessmen, a large amount of income tax evasion, an increasing rate of juvenile delinquency, an increase in all sorts of crimes including forcible rape, 17,000 people killed annually by guns, and 50,000, on the highways. This is a harsh indictment of American life. We must ask ourselves what role religion is to play if we hope to build the spiritual core of our country to meet the urgent problems we face in the second half of the twentieth century. Clearly, if organized religion is to survive, it must become more interested in problems of social change—and quickly. Our society needs a unique type of social institution which is flexible and capable of a high level of intelligent self-direction on the part of its adherents. Can the church meet the challenge, or will the school gradually become the social organization that will effect beneficial social change?

RELIGION AND PHYSICAL EDUCATION

Relatively few significant historical studies have been conducted within our field relative to the influence of religion on physical education and sport, although there is some evidence that this situation will be changed shortly. Other historians have occasionally provided insight into this question, and with their help we can turn to many fine sources still available. It is true that in the early cultures the so-called physical and mental education of the people could not be viewed separately. Many ancient rituals and ceremonies included a variety of types of dance and physical exercise that may well have contributed to physical endurance and skill. The development of these attributes may have been incidental, or it may have been by actual design on the part of the priests and elders.

Various early religions placed great stress on a life of quiet contemplation, and this may well have contributed to the disesteem of certain bodily activities of a physical nature. Continuing emphasis on intellectual attainment for certain classes in various societies must have strengthened this attitude. Yet the harmonious ideal of the Athenians had aesthetic and religious connotations that cannot be denied, and physical education and sport ranked high in this scheme. The same cannot be said for the practical-minded Romans, however, where the "sound mind in a sound body" concept meant that the body was well trained for warlike pursuits and other activities of a similar nature.

Despite considerable writing in our field to the effect that the Christian Church was responsible for the low status of physical education, recreation, and athletics in the Western world, some evidence to the contrary is now accumulating. It is seemingly true that Christian idealism furthered the dualism of mind and body—a concept the effects of which have been detrimental to physical activity ever since. Furthermore, the doctrine of original sin, with the possibility of ultimate salvation if asceticism were practiced, tended to negate the fostering of the Greek ideal for well over a thousand years. H. I. Marrou (1964, pp. 185–86) takes the opinion, however, that "physical education was quite dead in the Christian era and that its death had been a natural one, unaccompanied by any violent revolution—history would have told us if there had been anything of the kind." He believes that the Church Fathers limited their harsh criticism to professional sport, not to amateur sport or physical education. This thesis is borne out by Ballou (1965), who comes to the conclusion that "early Christianity taught that God cared about bodies as well as souls in contrast to a position suggested by physical literature that God only cared about souls." He explains further that the "body-is-evil" approach was generated by proponents of heretical movements later rejected by the Church. Ballou concludes, however, that the Christian Church "failed to exert leadership in the area of the games by not reorienting them to a Christian perspective." Until further corroborative study clarifies this matter from different aspects over a longer period of time, we may tentatively conclude that the earlier blame placed upon the Church itself will have to be tempered.

The fact still remains, however, that physical education and "the physical" did fall into disrepute, until certain humanistic educators revived the Greek ideal during the Renaissance. The mind-body dichotomy has plagued both this field and the entire theory of education. Even today, when the unity of the human organism has become common knowledge and is continually being substantiated by new evidence, this unfortunate situation persists. Insofar as the churches are concerned, however, the situation has been gradually improving in the past one hundred years. It could be argued that spreading materialism has weakened the influence of religion and that church leaders are acceding to the popularity of physical recreation in order to maintain their congregations. It seems reasonable to conclude, however, that organized religion, and certainly specific denominations within the major organized religions, is becoming increasingly aware of the role that physical recreation can play in the promulgation of the Christian idealistic way of life.

To substantiate this statement, a few examples will be presented. Bennett pointed out that The Church of Jesus Christ of Latter-Day Saints, of all the various religions and denominations, appears to be taking the strongest position in regard to the care of the body, inasmuch as "the Mormon faith teaches that the spirit and body are the soul of man. It looks upon the body as a non-evil component of the eternal soul of man. . . ." Bennett, himself a Presbyterian, believes strongly that recreation under religious sponsorship can help the American people improve moral and ethical standards; except for the Mormons, however, he sees few significant signs of encouragement among most Protestant churches.

Still further, organized Christianity has taken the role of sport much more seriously in recent years as well. Another indication of Christianity's new interest in sport has been the establishment and rapid development of the Fellowship of Christian Athletes. This is an organization which "exists to serve Christ and the Church. Its concern is to draw athletes in particular and youth in general into the realm and experience of vital Christian commitment within the Church" (1962).

One further quotation made by the late Pope Pius XII (1945) shows the type of support he gave to athletics: ". . . Now, what is primarily the duty and scope of sports, wholesomely and Christianly understood, if not to cultivate the dignity and harmony of the human body, to develop health, strength, agility, and grace? . . ."

CONCLUSION

Thus, it appears that various religious leaders at different stages in the world's history have exerted a variety of influences on health education, physical education, recreation, and sport. It is evident, however, that much more careful study of this question is in order, especially since modern psychology has placed increasing emphasis on man's indivisibility into mind and matter. The more essentialistic philosophies of education have typically established a hierarchy of values ignoring the importance of a well-rounded education, despite the fact that lip service is regularly paid to the necessity for man's physical, as well as mental, culture. Interestingly enough, even many pragmatic naturalists and experimentalists do not in practice accord physical education and play what they claim are their rightful places in the education of youth. Yet those of us in this field professionally should not despair; we are making definite progress in so many ways, and scientific evidence is accumulating to such a degree that value systems may in time be changed, or at least altered considerably. It seems reasonable to say that Christianity and Judaism have hampered the fullest development of physical, health, and recreation education, but it is true also that many of these religious leaders are revamping their earlier positions as they realize the potential of these activities as spiritual forces in man's life. And the world is marching on. . . .

IV

The
Professional
Viewpoint

Whereas the earlier problems presented can be classified as social forces influencing the whole field of education, those included in this chapter have a much greater professional orientation. Of course, these problems have also been influenced by social forces.

section one

METHODS OF INSTRUCTION

Any educational curriculum has been, and is continually, influenced by a variety of political, economic, philosophical, religious, and scientific factors. In curriculum construction, therefore, a primary task is to determine which subjects should be included because of the *recurring* interest among educators and laymen for their inclusion at some level of the educational system. In an earlier chapter treating values and aims, curriculum development was presented in historical perspective. Today, as always in the history of man, decisions must be made as to how a curriculum is selected. Shall its construction be based on the philosophy of state and its function, on the demands of nationalism, on whether it will help man to make a better living, on whether it will help him to stay alive and healthy, on the need for reduction of tension in a troubled world, on the nature of man, *or* according to the way in which he learns best? Or is there perhaps a predetermined set of values that dictates educational aims? We must ask ourselves further whether the educator's task is to transmit the cultural heritage, to help youth develop skills for problem solving, or to provide a miniature society in which students may enjoy "living at its best" so that they will have an example to follow in their after school days. If we view the curriculum as a means of disciplining the mind, we will tend to stress certain time-proven subjects. If, on the other hand, we want to help youth develop a number of habit patterns that will be effective in his social environment, certain other subject matter areas or experiences will be included. The curriculum has developed and expanded at a fantastic rate in the United States, and many people insist that this trend must be reversed so that the "essential" subjects can be taught adequately.

BRIEF HISTORICAL BACKGROUND

Primitive and preliterate man undoubtedly learned through imitation and through trial and error. When writing developed in the early civilizations, memorization played a large part in the educational process. Tradition and custom were highly regarded, and the importance of precept and proper example were important aspects of both physical and mental culture. Testing in early societies was carried out through various initiatory ceremonies designed to give the young man (and occasionally the young woman) the opportunity to test himself in the presence of his peers and elders. Most of the education seems to have been informal, however, and different systems of apprenticeship were employed in all phases of life's activities. The educational pattern was prescribed, and the young people were expected to follow the same traditions and customs from generation to generation. The practical aspects of life were learned by doing them repeatedly, and strict discipline was often employed if the child were lazy or recalcitrant.

In early Greece many of the same methods were used, and motivation was supplied by introducing elements of rivalry as well as by narration of various tales and myths of the great heroes of the past. In Spartan Greece, boys were taken from their homes at the age of seven years, and their training in the barracks was in the hands of very strict captains. The educational program was severe and exacting, as the ultimate aim was the production of a brave and hardened soldier. Officers of the state examined these boys and young men regularly. Incompetence and cowardice were grounds for punishment by flogging, and there is no doubt but that the element of fear can encourage a certain type of learning.

The educational methods of the early Athenians were similar but, according to popular belief, not quite as strict and harsh as those of the Spartans. There was no question, however, but that lax methods would produce poor results. Attention was given to the grouping of young men according to capacity, and there was evidently very careful matching for the various contests that were sponsored regularly. Overemphasis in coaching and the development of certain specialized techniques became a distinct problem in later Athens, and this trend was often criticized by philosophers and other educational leaders.

Roman education was extremely utilitarian in nature. In the early Roman period such education was centered in the family, although its ultimate goal was service to the state. These children learned by precept and example from their parents and elders. Obedience was at times exacted through an extremely rigorous discipline. Parents gave their children regular supervision and made every effort to set fine examples for them; the child was expected to "do the thing that was to be done." The cultural aspects of the educational process, so evident in later Athenian education, were almost completely lacking in early Rome. Later, as the need for higher intellectual attainments developed, the task of educating the child often fell to Greek slaves. Thus the Romans made no significant innovations in educational method and indeed failed even to appreciate two areas where the Greeks had excelled—music and gymnastics.

The Christian Church dominated the educational scene in the early Middle Ages. Although Jesus of Nazareth is generally regarded as a great religious leader and a fine teacher, many of those who followed him employed less exciting teaching methods. Jesus is said to have taught with enthusiasm and authority. He had a commanding knowledge of Jewish history and lore, and yet he dealt with the controversial issues of the time. He welcomed questions from his audience, and he made full use of his excellent powers of persuasion. Many less capable Church leaders in the early Middle Ages, however, evidently employed a great deal of formality and dogmatism in their teaching. St. Augustine (354–430 A.D.) attempted to put more life into his teaching methods and those of his associates, but educational methods generally seem to have been dominated by asceticism and severe discipline. However, the training of monks and knights necessarily included a fair share of realism and practicality.

Educational methodology is said to have improved considerably toward the end of the Middle Ages when the universities were gaining in power and prestige. The Catholic Church made an effort to combine the best of Aristotle's approach to teaching with the better methodology employed in Christian education. St. Thomas Aquinas placed great stress on what might be called the self-activity of the learner. Debating techniques and Aristotelian logic were employed to stimulate interest and to promote sound learning. Of course, the lecture method was still most prominent, as printing had not yet been invented. Subsequently, the idea of the dissertation was introduced—the hypothesis and the findings were defended orally.

With the onset of the Renaissance, there was greater recognition of individual differences. Vittorino da Feltre, who conducted the school at the Court of the Prince of Mantua, encouraged the idea of small classes in which the child's needs and capacities were considered. To him self-activity was very important, as well as consistent use of constructive criticism and praise. The whole spirit of this period was humanistic, and it is not surprising that innovations were employed to make the process more interesting to all concerned. The reader should not be misled, however, into thinking that school work had become fun; lectures and disputations were still the most frequent teaching methods at the university level, and the students at the lower levels were largely involved in memorization and emulation.

This discussion of the historical background of educational methodology could be prolonged indefinitely; many famous educational leaders since the Renaissance have made significant contributions, but their influence was often short-lived and they themselves were often dominated by social forces beyond their immediate control. For us as physical educators it is important to understand that the concept of a mind-body dualism has prevailed in many quarters down to the present day, despite the evidence from psychology about the unity of the human organism. Fortunately, gradual realization has come that people learn in many ways, not just *"intellectually"*; but observations of various classes on all levels even today are often discouraging in this regard.

In the eighteenth and nineteenth centuries, educators like Rousseau, Froebel, Pestalozzi, and Herbart, working with preadolescents, set the stage for the investigations and subsequent innovations of the twentieth century. Unfortunately, most of us still "do not teach as well as we know how," either in the classroom or in the gymnasium and the pool. The social forces at work today have resulted in a new drive toward the mastery of facts and knowledge, and at the same time in physical education we are exhorted to provide physical fitness so that a "sound mind can be superimposed on a sound body." Thus, we continue to come full circle to the question of educational philosophy, and whether chemistry, for example, is essential in the curriculum and physical education is nonessential. Some would argue that we should take advantage of the "current winds" of essentialism and stress the physical *training* aspects of our work in order to insure our place in the daily school program.

Is physical education "curricular," "cocurricular," or "extracurricular?" Your answer to this question may well depend upon your position on the educational philosophy spectrum (see p. 42). Thinking about the entire field of physical, health, and recreation education (and this includes safety and driver education, as well as intramural and interscholastic athletics), the experimentalist will see it as "curricular"; the realist, as "extracurricular," with the possible exception of a daily "physical training" period; and the idealist, as "cocurricular."

Having taken this stand, we must come to a decision as to the influence that content has on method. Shall physical, health, and recreation education (or whatever part of it you would include in the curriculum) be taught formally, semiformally, or informally? Our primary concern as teachers is motivating the student so that the learning process will occur most easily and the material will be remembered most thoroughly. Or looking at it another way, What are the most effective means whereby the teacher can get the student to perform a physical skill most efficiently in keeping with his potential? Or from still another standpoint, What is the best way for the teacher to arrange the learning situation so that the student may modify his ways of behaving and truly understand what he is doing? In offering some answers to these questions from various standpoints on the educational philosophy spectrum, we should keep in mind that teachers generally, no matter what their philosophy, have been increasingly sensitive to changes in psychological learning theory.

PHILOSOPHICAL ANALYSIS

The *experimentalist* is chiefly concerned with aims that emerge out of the educative process; objectives and teaching methods must go hand in hand to be most effective. Experimentalistic teachers should be characterized by a social outlook that is broad, by special consideration for the learner, by a fine background of educational preparation, and by teaching techniques that are planned specifically for the teaching situation at hand. A physical education program which is interesting and significant to the student is the only way that his attention can be guaranteed. With this in mind, therefore, teachers should begin at the student's level and give him as much freedom as he can use wisely. This will mean that there will be opportunities for changes in plan and program often involving student choice.

If we involve the student in purposeful activity just as soon as possible, the learning experience will be greatly improved. Disciplinary measures, if necessary at all, should arise spontaneously from the actions of the class. The experimentalist rejects measurement of student progress by an absolute standard; he is vitally concerned however with evaluation of individual pupil growth, and especially with the student's self-evaluation of the success or failure of the whole educational venture.

Authoritative use of texts and preplanned lectures do not fit into the experimentalist's teaching program, one of the reasons being that experimental problem solving involves a considerable measure of contingency. An experimentalistic teacher guides his students in such a way that they will use their reasoning abilities in the realization of the technical, associated, and concomitant learnings available to them as they learn the various sport skills.

Before we move toward the center and right side of the educational philosophy spectrum, let's take a quick look at the *reconstructionist's teaching method*. As you will recall, this has been designated by some as the "extreme" progressivistic position. Typically, this is a group-centered approach to education in which majority decisions prevail. The main aim of education is to "reconstruct" society and to "internationalize" the democratic ideal throughout the world. With this approach, therefore, all teaching methods should be geared to the realization of the agreed-upon goals. Learning is a cooperative venture, and the interest of the student is obtained by providing purposeful activity consistent with the educational goals. The teacher assumes the role of a democratic leader as he guides students who must assume responsibility if progress toward social self-realization is ever to be made. Discipline, if and when necessary, comes from the group. Tests are shared efforts; awards and prizes are not made to individuals, as the emphasis is placed upon group accomplishment; and in place of necessarily subjective grades is a conference to evaluate the student's total growth.

A consideration of *realistic teaching method* brings us to the essentialistic side of the educational philosophy spectrum. Here there are typically two orders of learning: a logical or "essential" order, and an order where the teacher starts with the child's interest and then works his way back to ensure what for him is adequate coverage of the subject matter. Generally speaking, "learning is a process of acquiring objective knowledge by the scientific method." One essentialist stresses that education is more than a matter of merely acquiring knowledge, since it must be used practically for subsequent enjoyment of life. The naturalistic realist typically practices a problem-solving approach to classroom learning, while, for the rational humanist, the greater the amount of reasoning required to learn a subject, the more important is that subject in the curriculum.

Realists support the theory of transfer of training; rational humanists and perennialists (scholastic realists) believe that this takes place through the transference of disciplinary values, which have a functional application to any situation. Furthermore, when a new learning situation presents itself, it is quite apt to contain a number of identical elements that had appeared earlier in another learning circumstance.

Interest is "desirable but subordinate to effort," and prizes and awards may be used by the teacher to stimulate students to achieve the greatest amount of excellence in their efforts. The curriculum, logically and sequentially arranged, presents little opportunity for electives; and drill, needed to perfect patterns of habit formation, especially at the lower learning levels, may, however, be varied and correlated with other teaching techniques.

The realistic teacher will find it legitimate to indoctrinate; the teacher is a "person of authority who transmits the truth and wisely guides immature minds." Another assessment of his role is that "the teacher should be the voice of science; clear, objective, and factual." He relies on proven methodology, and the application of research and measurement to physical education is most important to him. He believes typically that there should be a physical education requirement throughout the years of the formal educational system—or at least until certain objective standards of performance are met.

Realists believe in the use of required texts which include all the necessary knowledge to be learned (of a theoretical nature). Quizzes and examinations are needed to convey to the student information about the calibre of his performance. Objective grades give students a clear appraisal of their progress and relative position in regard to others.

Much of what has been said about realistic teaching method applies to the classroom situation, of course, and implications for physical training can be logically assumed. The teacher should organize his gymnasium period to guarantee muscle development, improvement of circulo-respiratory efficiency, and increased coordination. The achievement of these objectives will require careful attention to the methodology discussed above. In the teaching of physical skills, furthermore, careful analysis will be necessary, as the whole process must be broken down into its elements and the interrelations perceived. The realistic teacher should be a movement analysis expert.

The *idealist* subordinates method to objectives; he is apt to state that he follows no one method wholly, but that he determines his own method as he progresses toward the realization of his immediate educational objective. Even Plato stressed that the teacher should not be particularly conscious as to whether he was using a specific technique. Rather, he believed that the teacher should use his reason and should base his selection of a particular activity or teaching technique on a foundation of sound scientific investigation with demonstrated validity and proper psychological methodology.

Idealists typically believe that students, with *careful guidance,* should choose their objectives, activities, topics for reports, and even their textbooks. Objective and subjective data gathered should be used for individual guidance and for group planning. They are also strong advocates of the use of the lives and works of great leaders to provide enrichment for the curriculum of the younger generation. Because children are such imitators, such a technique will encourage them to strive for high attainment.

Interest is most important, but the idealist has discovered that it alone will not suffice to accomplish all the necessary educational objectives. Although a play attitude is especially good with children, the instructor should not forget that time-proven proverb that "the hard is the good." Furthermore, when discipline is invoked to cause the student to respond with effort, he may well discover in a short while that his interest has been aroused.

An idealist believes that bodily development is limited to the unfolding of what is given the individual by birth, since education cannot augment the nerve cells of the brain. It can, however, fully develop any capacities for which there is potentiality within the student. For this reason it is important to help children get the right start in health and physical education. They should become as skillful as possible, have a reasonable amount of success, and have a lot of fun in physical activity.

The idealistic coach will point out to aspiring young athletes that they will have to make certain sacrifices if they hope to be successful and worthy team members. Interscholastic sport competition provides a dramatic means of contributing to individual development, as it develops traits of perseverance, courage, and respect for law and order. The coach should eventually step into the background as his boys achieve maturity. The goal is not glory for the coach; it is presumably to help the participants achieve their inherent selfhood. The coach with a truly idealistic philosophy will make every effort to keep from succumbing to the materialistic demands of the public. In athletics we should do all in our power to avoid extreme specialization within the educational system, because the development of the whole personality of the participant is apt to suffer when the performance of the skill becomes most important.

The idealistic teacher of physical education should not only be able to teach specific skills; he must be aware of ever-present opportunities for developing related interests. The rigidly formal physical education class, the stereotyped, dull team practice, or the gymnasium activity which is often merely poorly organized informal recreation will be avoided if the teacher uses a method that creates some suspense for the student—"suspense to be resolved only by his own decision or active effort."

In physical education theory or health instruction in the classroom, the teacher would be wise to use an "informal dialectic" that encourages the student to think about the problem under discussion. Some lecturing and experimenting can be useful along with the discussion technique. The idealistic teacher must constantly remind himself that his influence is making an impact on man's mind and spirit, that, accordingly, his teaching should serve human needs and help others understand Christian principles.

The existentialist's possible teaching method is difficult to conceptualize. In the first place, he is primarily concerned that the young person should have the opportunity to grow in an environment of freedom—no choices should ever be forced on the student! He would agree, for example, that a democratic learning situation is better than an essentialistic one; yet, even in the democratic environment a person may be deprived of the opportunity to make his own individual decision. Any design for education that is superimposed on the developing student tends to rob him of his chance to be his own unique self.

Thus, the very fact that a teacher is provided in the school situation means that he must employ extreme care in the educational methodology that he practices on the often unsuspecting child. As the existentialist sees it, it is up to the teacher to insert a moral dimension into the child's education. This is *not* meant to imply that the teacher should make any moral decisions for the child. To the contrary, the essential task is merely to give the child an awareness of himself in relation to the world, to provide an impartial background for decision making. He should not be made to fit into some preestablished system of what is right or wrong, or be told how he should solve the problems he will encounter in an overly socialized environment.

THE ROLE OF
ADMINISTRATION

As our society continues to grow in complexity, amazing social changes are taking place. The continuing Industrial Revolution, coupled with literally fantastic advances in science and technology, has placed man in our most modern societies in a most difficult situation. These factors, along with the exploding population and the resultant development of immense urban and suburban areas, have created a situation in which a certain percentage of the manpower has been forced to concern itself increasingly with the management of the efforts of the large majority of the people in our society. The ability of a relatively few individuals to master this task to a reasonable degree has meant that the world as we know it could continue to grow and develop. This is not meant to imply that a great many people have not organized and administered all types of enterprises in the various aspects of life in the past. The point here is that most recently an "organizational" or "administrative revolution" has taken place, and will continue to take place, because of the extreme complexity of our evolving society. Thus, it is administrative theory and/or thought that is relatively new rather than administrative practice. Such practice, closely related to the broad processes of historical evolution, has been affected by the many social forces at work during these centuries.

general historical background

Social organizations, of one type or another, are inextricably related to man's history as a human and social animal. In the early societies there were family units, clans, and tribes. Superior-subordinate relationships evolved according to the very nature of things, as man produced goods, fought wars, organized his society politically, formed his churches, and developed a great variety of formal and informal associations. In certain eras these organizations within the various groups and communities became very large. They grew, changed, developed further, changed their functions along the way, and then, in most cases vanished as the particular civilization declined. The central theme seems to have been that of *change*—change that was made to strengthen the organization, change that meant more and perhaps better administration as the organizations grew. If power is required to accomplish a given task in a certain way, then people must be organized and programs must be administered to foster the desired development. Generally speaking, and this statement can be misinterpreted, the more formal the organizational structure is, the more power can be summoned to effect the desired goals. Leaders use money to bring about the necessary combination of human and physical resources (*i.e.,* the power) to get the job done. Still further, as these resources are combined in various ways, many different and improved techniques are developed which may hasten the end result. Somehow social change takes place as people develop the desire, the physical resources, and the technical know-how to perform the task in the most expedient manner possible. The desire, of course, originates from the ideals and values of the culture—values that aid the leaders in attitude formation.

In a recent, truly monumental study, Gross traces the historical development of administrative thought (1964). He points out that it was only recently that "administrative thought emerged as a differentiated field of sustained writing, conscious observation, abstract theory, and specialized terminology" (p. 91). He explains how rulers in ancient times were expected to be wise, good, bold, willing to compromise, unscrupulous, and well-advised. Still further, various plans of administrative education were developed as formal organizations grew. Then more recently after the Industrial Revolution really gathered momentum, certain basic changes began to take place in what might be called "administrative technology." It was subsequently accompanied by larger organizations with more subdivisions, directed by more administrators, creating a greater amount of bureaucracy.

EDUCATIONAL ADMINISTRATION

The American people have always had faith in education as the guardian of a democratic government, as probably the best assurance of a forward-looking society, and as an open door to every person for the realization of his potential abilities. Education has become a tremendous public business, with the normal community using over one-half of its tax money for schools. It is estimated that over forty million people have some direct connection with public education, not to mention private education statistics. The business of education will continue to grow; with an ever expanding population and still unmet challenges, it would be folly to predict otherwise. The school has truly been a remarkable social experiment in the United States, but it must keep abreast of social needs for continued progress.

There is a definite need for efficient administration based on sound theory and scientific evidence in such a large business-like organization as the modern school. The many problems presented continually to administrators involve a seemingly unending chain of details, and the tempo of school life is steadily increasing. The well-prepared and ethical school administrator is ultimately responsible for the efficient performance of a myriad of duties. It is very important for him to realize that his position and resultant functions exist as a *means* to an end. American education will always need more and better qualified administrators.

Administration has undergone a process of gradual evolution that parallels the growth of the school system itself. Originally no one even thought of administrators and school board members in our schools. The school was administered democratically by the people at town meetings. As towns grew this became impractical, and town selectmen were delegated the responsibility. In 1827 Massachusetts became the first state to enact a law requiring towns to have separate committees for the schools. Ten years later the first superintendency was created in Providence, Rhode Island. New York had had a state superintendent in 1812. The functions of the early superintendents were only vaguely defined, because the boards of education refused to recognize their professional status. It took a full century for school boards to accord the superintendent his rightful function as a professional expert in the area of school management.

There has been a parallel development at the college and university level. The creation of a board of overseers and a corporation at Harvard College in 1642 and 1650, respectively, pointed the way for democratic administration in higher education in the United States. There have been variations in form, but the principle of centralized administrative authority exists in almost all American colleges and universities today. The administration is responsible to a group outside the school, the composition of which varies according to the source of financial support.

It is often not understood that, by constitutional law, the individual state has the power to make adequate education available to its citizens. Much of this power, along with the necessary details for execution of the school program, has been delegated to the local community. The members of local school boards can never be allowed to forget, however, that they are acting as agents of the state. Basically, the functions of school administration are legislative, executive, and inspectorial; the board's function is to legislate with the aid of professional guidance. Individual board members, therefore, are an elected group who see to it that the schools are operated efficiently. A board should have rules and regulations as to its functions, organization, and responsibilities. A large part of the superintendent's job is to advise the board in such a way that the group functions harmoniously. As individuals, board members have no power to act, and they should never assume executive duties; their power to legislate the conduct of the schools stems from group action only. The board represents the public; it legislates, it employs, and it appraises the status of education in the local community.

In this way our pattern of education has developed. The superintendent of schools acts as a "professional guide" to the board of education. Upon his recommendation, the board employs school principals, who hopefully will display many of the same characteristics an excellent superintendent possesses. The principal is the professional representative of the superintendent in a particular school. He receives his authority either verbally or in writing, which makes him the agent of the board of education. Ideally, there should be rules and regulations which govern the principal's position. Merely stating that "the principal shall be responsible for the efficient operation of his school" seemingly allows for too broad an interpretation on the part of this executive. In the professional relationship of principal and teacher, a correct understanding and full appreciation of the role of each is extremely important. Both should understand that they are co-workers in a common enterprise with joint responsibility for the pupil.

When the term "administration" is used in education, it is usually associated with such words as superintendence, direction, management, planning, supervision, organization, regulation, guidance, and control. In common usage we think of it as the process of directing people in an endeavor. This function is carried out in a variety of ways by many people in the field of physical, health, and recreation education. The typical approach to administration is to ascertain those principles and operational policies upon which we can base our own theory and practice. Administration, in its simplest form, could probably be likened to a football coach blowing his whistle to call the players together at the beginning of practice. To carry this parallel further, it is obvious that the coaching of a football team involves different types of activity. The more complex the activity, the more specialization becomes necessary. Thus, the football coach, as an administrator, must devote long hours to planning, organization, coordination, and evaluation, in addition to his teaching functions of directing the operation on the basis of the plan thus evolved.

PHILOSOPHIES OF ADMINISTRATION

Traditionally, departments of physical education and/or athletics, just like other departments in a school, seem often to have operated on the basis of a group of unexpressed major and minor principles. Such principles, probably necessary to the proper formulation of operational policies, exist, explicitly or implicitly, beneath every specific act of teaching in a particular field. Still deeper, a consistent and logical philosophy of life and/or religion should be the foundation upon which at least the administrator or the majority of his department rests. Unfortunately, emergencies and practical considerations, as well as individual personalities and possibly conflicting administrative patterns, force a department almost constantly to make exceptions to its "prevailing" philosophy. At times, a program takes on the appearance of a patchwork that bears little resemblance to any common philosophy. For these reasons, it now seems logical to draw some inferences for prospective administrators from the leading philosophical tendencies. There are many who would immediately say that to do so in connection with *any* of the major philosophical positions would be skating on very thin ice indeed. It does seem, however, that every administrator needs such a framework of action and that he should get some guidance from these basic beliefs. If this is not possible, philosophy will continue to find its work taken over by newer disciplines.

experimentalism

The *experimentalistic approach to administration,* is, as revealed in the persistent problems already discussed, basically open-minded and unbiased. The administrator makes every effort to conduct the affairs of the department as a democratic undertaking in which all the various individuals concerned have the opportunity to share in policy formation as well as the rest of the operation. Students and staff are not afraid to come to him with their problems, since his actions are "in keeping with his words." When he does criticize any staff member or student, it is done in such a way that a minimum of antagonism occurs. The individual concerned is encouraged to present his side of the story. The end result should be that the person leaves with a desire to improve his performance to live up to the confidence the administrator has placed in him.

The experimentalistic administrator encourages both staff and students to offer constructive criticisms in a variety of ways. All departmental policy is decided through democratic procedure. The administrator sees himself as a chairman at meetings. He may well speak to the various issues and problems at hand, perhaps without the formality of leaving the chair. His "democracy-in-action" approach is quite apparent throughout the program and is reflected in the attitudes of the staff and the students toward the enterprise. A staff member given responsibility finds that the authority to carry it out is present as well. Such an administrator treats his staff members as co-workers. He encourages staff study projects and wants all staff members to improve themselves professionally. When staff members do something that merits praise, this man sees that their work is recognized both within and without the department.

Through the best possible personal relationships the experimentalistic administrator creates an atmosphere in which all can make a full contribution to the progress of the department. If such an administrator resigns his position, it would not be unusually difficult for a qualified staff member to assume the chairman's position. A successor does not have to learn the tricks of the trade through bitter experience.

Such an administrator realizes that among the many relations and determinants that influence a person's behavior in any given situation emotional acceptance rates high. He views administration as a developing social science. He knows that he can't expect cooperation on the part of all concerned to develop by chance so he seeks to involve all staff members in policy formation and to keep the lines of communication open. In this way there is a much greater possibility that the goals of democratic, experimental education will be realized.

realism

A *realistic approach to administrative control* is entirely predictable. The administrator, possessing ultimate responsibility, makes decisions affecting the rest of the staff and the students. "Authority is therefore centralized in a line-staff pattern of control" (Morland, 1958, p. 295). The administrator tends to function as a business executive who has been hired to make wise, clearcut decisions when the situation so warrants. The administrator may ask staff members for opinions; and he may have committees investigate certain problems and come up with recommendations. But the eventual decision is up to him. As one investigator stated: "As an administrator my decisions are dictated by the impersonal results of objective experimentation. However, I stand ready to modify procedures as more effective methods are established." The school board, which retains ultimate responsibility, typically delegates the administrator a certain amount of responsibility commensurate with the authority granted him to get the job done. The teacher has little choice but to carry out the directions of his superior, no matter what his personal feelings may be. The realist feels such administrative theory is compatible with life in an evolving democracy, because there will always be "some chiefs and many Indians." Someone has to call the shots, bear the brunt of the responsibility, and accept the rewards or suffer the consequences. The idea of taking a vote to get majority opinion before any departmental action is taken may sound good in theory, but it does not centralize the responsibility on one pair of shoulders, and may well result in nothing but "pooled ignorance" concerning a controversial issue. Basically, it is simply not a very *realistic* approach! Besides, it is humanly impossible in large organizations to take time to have a vote on everything. School boards, as one unit of control, should hire administrators, set policy, back up decisions made by administrators in line with such policy, reward them if their "batting averages" on decisions are quite high, and fire them if they prove to be incompetent.

idealism

The idealistic educator faces a predicament that he must resolve in order to reach a logical and consistent administrative policy. On the one hand, idealism is a strongly essentialistic philosophy of education. Because of an absolute moral law in the universe, and because education's aim is to help the child adjust to the fundamental realities disclosed by history, idealists firmly believe it necessary to conserve and transmit the established value pattern. On the other hand, idealistic philosophy of education places great emphasis on the freedom, growth, and development of the personality. Despite his "will to perfection," the idealist is most concerned with instilling the skills and techniques necessary to social responsiveness. If we hope to develop the correct attitudes in children, they must come indirectly "by example, inspiration, and contagion" (Zeigler, 1964, pp. 237–38). This leads us to the view that the personality of the teacher is tremendously important! In the idealistic tradition, great teachers and leaders have respect for the student's personality and intelligence. The ideal teacher does not superimpose his will on others. He does not demand respect; he earns it by his manner and bearing. As a good friend to the pupils in his classes, he has a keen desire to show them what democratic living is like, because he realizes that they in turn will help to democratize others. Is it too much, therefore, to suggest that there are many implications here for the idealistic administrator—to hope that an improved type of democracy in educational administration will some day become a reality despite the line-staff pattern of control apparently a hallmark of essentialistic educational philosophy?

CONCLUSION

To draw this discussion to a close, we can broadly state that the *essentialist* believes in certain inviolable theoretical principles of administration. These principles provide many answers to administrative problems and can greatly help the neophyte. An essentialist would tend to administer a program by "the seat of his pants," so to speak. He would view administration as an art, not a science. He would argue that many fine administrators have never had a course in administration, and that such courses would not help significantly. In general, he approves of the practice, in higher education especially, of selecting administrators from the ranks of scholars and/or research scientists, who will then learn to administer an educational organization on the job.

The *progressivist,* and many social scientists, tends to believe that no practical rules exist which can be applied in an automatic fashion to the organizational problems which actually arise. He would view administration as a developing social (behavioral) science; that is, an area where scientific evidence about man and his interrelationships with others can provide important keys to the decision-making process. If a person is aware of these new developments and has had an internship experience, it seems to the progressivist that he will have a much better chance of becoming a successful administrator—all other things being equal. The argument here is that an administrator's practice should be based on the ever-increasing knowledge available to us through the behavioral sciences particularly (within the larger number of social sciences). Then it is a question of employing this knowledge skillfully to the task at hand.

section three

THE HEALTHY BODY

Although we discussed attitudes toward the place of health education (in *all* of its aspects) within the educational system briefly in the first chapter, they are of such importance today that they merit special consideration as a separate persistent problem.

The condition of his body has undoubtedly always been of concern to man. Early man found that a certain type of fitness was necessary for life. As Dr. Steinhaus of George Williams College has indicated in many of his earlier analyses of this subject, man's muscles, including his heart, *had* to be strong; his vision *had* to be keen; and he *had* to be able to run fast. Physical efficiency was necessary for survival. Modern man, more successful than his prehistoric brother in making an adjustment to his environment, lives longer. He has had the experience of his forefathers upon which to base his judgments. His success is dependent, however, on complicated procedures. His teeth depend upon competent dentistry. His eyes very often depend on the services of highly trained opthamologists, oculists, optometrists, and opticians. Highly qualified medical doctors and surgeons preserve the health of his heart, lungs, and other vital organs. Protruding neck, round shoulders, sagging abdomen, and pronated ankles (including "flat" feet) are indirectly results of the machine age. His heart pounds wildly when he runs fifty yards after a departing bus or subway train, or when he climbs a flight of stairs fairly rapidly. Often he has difficulty adjusting his elemental emotions to the habit pattern of "do's and don'ts" that we commonly term civilization. When this occurs, and it is occurring with increasing regularity, modern man cracks under the strain and is referred to a hospital as another victim of what has been designated as psychosomatic difficulties.

HISTORICAL BACKGROUND

A study of past and present civilizations indicates that the sociological states of war and peace produce quite different health emphases. Freedom from disqualifying defects, strength, and endurance are important to men who want to win wars. When a particular war is over, the society is then able to focus its attention again toward the mastery of its own environment. During such periods the emphasis in health can be placed on the related questions of man's longevity and environmental health.

There has always been a great deal of ignorance about sound health practices throughout the world. However, attempts at scientific solutions may be dated as long ago as 1000 B.C. with the Egyptians. These people tried to curtail the spread of communicable disease through land drainage and also developed some primitive pharmaceutical knowledge. The Hebrews extended somewhat the health knowledge of the Egyptians in the areas of water purification, waste disposal, food protection, communicable disease control, and maternity care, certain elements of which were incorporated into the Mosaic Law.

The Greeks regarded hygiene, the science of preserving health, as a positive goal. The Spartans preserved the lives of the healthy, strong infants and exposed the unfit to die on Mount Taygetus. These hardy youth were then subject to a most rigorous existence in preparation for military service. The Athenians, with a much broader educational aim, sought to realize sound personal health for Athenian youth through improved nutrition, a variety of types of exercise, and plenty of fresh air. They were fortunate to have Hippocrates, the father of medicine, as a physician who made a sound effort to place medicine on a scientific basis. He saw prevention as medicine's true ideal. Basically, he classified the causes of disease into those brought on by external conditions such as climate and those caused by internal conditions such as lack of exercise and poor health habits. Unfortunately most of this "knowledge" was based upon false premises which were not corrected until many hundreds of years later with the beginnings of the science of bacteriology. We do have the Greeks to thank, however, for the ideal of the sound body developed through their recommended program of "health gymnastics."

The Romans adopted many of the advances the Greeks had made, although they were basically suspicious of them as foreigners. The only significant forward step in public health made by the Romans seems to have been in the area of sanitary engineering. The city of Rome had a well-organized sewer system and a tremendous aqueduct (as did many other cities in the Empire). Military hospitals were evidently constructed in a sanitary manner as well. Even though Rome's location and the actual environment have been called "healthful" by some, there is evidence of a number of epidemics, especially during the flooding periods and the warmer season of the year. As the Roman economy improved, the dangers of over-eating became a problem for some. There was continuing concern that the people were not leading the same healthy lives they had in the earlier days. Writers of the time stressed the need for healthful exercises and recreational activities, especially for the sedentary, but often to no avail. Galen, a famous physician of the time, wrote a number of essays on the subject of healthful exercise, while deploring athletic contests that promoted excesses and often resulted in the maiming of participants. A type of early medical science began to develop with all sorts of specialization. Some of these physicians had talent, but many were quacks of the worst order. State medicine, encouraged by Caesar, ultimately vanished in the waning days of the Empire, mainly due to the pseudo-science of early Christian saints.

During the Middle Ages, the seemingly timeless Graeco-Roman civilization and culture all but disappeared, including the areas of public health and medical practice. Leprosy was one disease which spread all over Europe, but the rigid establishment of isolation camps eventually brought about its eradication. The recognition that the various communicable diseases were spread by contact with the infected persons was an important step taken in preventive medicine. A type of quarantine was even established for ships entering ports. It has been estimated that plagues and epidemics killed off approximately one-quarter of the population of the time. It is not surprising that people sought an explanation in God's wrath and other superstitious beliefs.

Many factors brought about a general awakening known as the Renaissance in the fourteenth century. A new spirit of inquiry that had been generally dormant for centuries arose. A rediscovery of the writings of Aristotle and the establishment of a number of universities helped to kindle a spirit of adventure and a desire to progress despite the existing sociological influences which made the era anything but peaceful. In the field of medicine Paracelsus (1491–1541) helped to liberate scientific thought from the formalized structure of Galen's teachings—medical treatises that had been written over a thousand years ago. Independent research and thought was greatly hampered by the status-quo attitude of both Church and State. Christianity in the Middle Ages must be credited, however, for the establishment of the first institutions that can be called hospitals. Saracenic learning, based to a considerable extent on Greek translations, no doubt helped to stimulate the awakening during the fifteenth and sixteenth centuries. Yet we find that surgery was still largely in the hands of barbers who worked in opposition to physicians and formed their own guild. One significant development during the sixteenth century was Ambroise Paré's surgical technique of tying an artery—a technique so necessary for successful amputations.

It would not serve our purpose to trace in detail at this point the various advances made in public health through the efforts of many great pioneers during the early modern period. Without their help we would not have the foundation upon which today's public health knowledge is based. Although the rate of progress may seem slow, an examination of the history of public health reveals that such advancement was often made despite adverse attitudes rather than with the help of public opinion. The period of the Industrial Revolution, for example, with the resultant urbanization and overcrowding, was a great challenge to those concerned. Fortunately, the changing political atmosphere encouraged governmental responsibility and made possible the advancement of humanitarian ideals. During the twentieth century there has been outstanding progress; nevertheless, it is profoundly disturbing that so many people in the world are still not able to profit to the fullest from these advances. In the United States a gigantic effort has been made to enlighten the public in the areas of personal and community health. The federal government has gradually assumed a larger role in the promotion of public health—this in the face of constant criticism that socialized medicine will help destroy our system of free enterprise.

Health education itself advanced rapidly after the stage had been set by the draft statistics of World War I. It was evident that many of these physical defects could have been prevented by proper measures taken during school years. Fortunately, money was available in the 1920s to do something about the situation.

Since that time many have concerned themselves with the development of school health education. Simultaneously, public health education in the home and community has advanced through the efforts of public and private agencies. During the 1920s, conflicting ideas arose as to the definition of health and the place of health instruction in the curriculum. Some people conceived of health as freedom from disease, while others saw it as an attribute of a strong, vigorous body. Still others have broadened this concept; the late Jesse Feiring Williams, for example, defined health as "that quality of life which enables the individual to live most and to serve best." According to this definition, the ultimate test of health is the use to which it is put.

implications from educational philosophy

Much of the disagreement as to the role of school health education in the educational pattern today stems from differing educational philosophies and from various concepts of "health." Perhaps the greatest hindrance to full acceptance of health education in the curriculum is the dualistic concept of man, first as a thinking being and only secondarily as a physical being.

For educational *progressivists,* sound health is one of the primary objectives of education, and the success of the school health education program depends upon the degree of cooperation among home, school, and community agencies. An educated person today must understand the difference between health and disease, and he should know how to protect and improve his own health, that of his dependents, and that of the community both large and small. In addition, physical training, health education, and instruction in profitable use of leisure time should be coordinated within the school program.

A school health education program designed to foster truly healthful living should be composed of three distinct, yet most closely related, divisions: 1) *healthful school living*—the development of the type of environment that will facilitate the optimal growth and development of students; 2) *health instruction*—a teaching program organized to develop specific knowledge, competencies, and attitudes concerning health; and 3) *health service*—provision for care when sudden illness or injury occurs, annual appraisal of health status, and health counseling including procedures for the prevention and/or control of communicable diseases.

The *realistic position* is not as clearcut in regard to the place of health education. Some realists view it naturalistically, while others take theological considerations into account. The naturalistic realist, for example, would state that he is concerned with maximum development of physical vigor and health, but the Thomist and rational humanist are inclined to preserve a certain hierarchy of values "inherent" in liberal education as they view it.

Broudy's position on the place of health education in the school structure (1961, pp. 149–171) appears to be fairly representative of the realist. He believes that the school *environment* should be healthy and that knowledge about the bases of emotional and physical health belongs in the curriculum. But from here on, other agencies should take up the task. The community, for example, has the responsibility of providing "clinical facilities for therapy," and the home must instill desirable health habits. He inquires further whether the school could ever hope to treat the matter of sex education adequately. In fact, Broudy even intimates that adolescents are for the most part so healthy that any discussion of health problems may seem unreal to them.

Perhaps the clearest statement of the *idealist's position* toward health and health education comes from the late Herman Harrell Horne. He omits it under a discussion of the "essential studies" in the curriculum except for incidental mention under biology, but then places "health" first in a list of nine basic values of human living. Horne explains this contradiction as follows: health education belongs at the bottom of the hierarchy of *educational* values, but the *quality* of health "enhances the richness of each and all of them (the other values)" (1942, p. 186).

Among Christian idealists, Mormons appear to take the strongest position in regard to the care of the body. According to their faith, the spirit and body *are* the soul of man. They conceive of the body as a non-evil component of man's eternal soul and look forward to literal resurrection after death. Thus, generally speaking, the idealist values a program of health and physical education highly as a service program which enables man to pursue still higher goals in education and in life.

The *existentialist*, as has been noted earlier, wants the school to help man become an authentic, self-determining individual. When the child realizes that he is responsible for his own conduct, education becomes for him a process of discovery. He *alone* can make the decision whether he needs to learn about personal and community health.

THE USE OF LEISURE

Citizens in the Western World now have more leisure than ever before, but the promotion of the concept of education for leisure depends a great deal on whether the prevailing educational philosophy will allow sufficient support for the inclusion of such programs in the educational system. When people achieve leisure, what will they do with it? What have they done with it in the past? Shall it be used for play, as typically conceived, or for recreation education? Our objective in this section is to trace the use of leisure throughout history and then to analyze how it *should* be used according to the major philosophical trends in Western educational philosophy.

As we begin this historical outline of the use of leisure, a few brief definitions seem to be in order. "Leisure" will be used to explain the time a person has free from his work and does not need for sleeping or basic survival activities. For our purposes we will accept the definition that play is an instinctive form of self-expression through pleasurable activity that seems to be aimless in nature. The term "recreation" seems to have developed a broader meaning than "play," although they are commonly used interchangeably by the layman. Typically, recreation embodies those experiences that people engage in during their leisure for purposes of pleasure, satisfaction, or education. Recreation is a human experience or activity; it is not necessarily instinctive; and it may be considered purposeful.

HISTORICAL BACKGROUND

In primitive and preliterate societies, there probably was not so sharp a division between work and play as in civilized societies. Grown-ups had a difficult time with basic survival activities and enjoyed very little leisure. Such leisure as a particular family or tribe was able to earn was probably used for play activity of an aimless nature, conjecturally quite similar to that of animals. Later, embryonic cultures developed certain folkways and ceremonials of a more controlled nature. Inclement weather, even in our own day, a mighty influence, may at least have afforded some leisure time.

A division of labor (with resultant leisure for some) occurred in Egypt, Mesopotamia, China, and India, generally considered the first great civilizations of the world. These social developments came about through favorable environments and men's correct responses to certain stimuli. The wealth accumulated through the toil of the masses was soon in the hands of a relatively few individuals; historically, these people were the first to enjoy anything like an extended period of leisure. Some used this free time to speculate and learn more about their environment; others developed various arts and skills, or participated in sports. Still others squandered the time in meaningless pursuits. In Egypt, for example, we find a great accumulation of formal knowledge that became available because religious leaders acquired wealth and leisure.

The Athenian Greeks developed a very high standard of living and, during their Golden Age, used their leisure wisely. Although Athenian democracy is often acclaimed as an ideal, the existence of three social classes (freemen, noncitizens, and slaves) must not be overlooked. Education was confined to native freemen, and Athenian women were regarded as inferior creatures to be kept on a low intellectual plane. Nevertheless, Athenians did have a revolutionary idea: a many-sided education, involving training of the mental, moral, physical, and aesthetic aspects of man's nature, an ideal the world had not seen before and has not been able to realize since then.

It has been said that the Romans never did more than merely perpetuate the Greek ideal of liberal education. Here again we find a stratification of society with the senators and the equites enjoying far greater wealth and social status than the plebeians; toward the end of the Republic there were as many as five million slaves in Italy. As usual, wealth determined leisure, and leisure determined the extent to which a man would be educated. Leisure was, in fact, synonymous with freedom.

How did the Romans use their leisure? Accumulated wealth led to unnecessary luxuries and selfish individualism. Social standing was determined to a large extent by the amount of one's personal fortune, and crass materialism became the leading philosophy of the time. Crime increased at all levels and often went unpunished. As the way of life changed for so many thousands of Romans, the formerly active Roman found himself unemployed and with no source of income. The state fed and entertained these people with great exhibitions, and a passion for the games and the circus grew. Many baths were provided for the physical recreation of the masses as well. Another strong factor in Rome's decline was the misuse of political power, by the senatorial class, which resulted in a series of civil wars just before Augustus came into power. What once had been an extremely strong state disintegrated as business men exploited the poor, civil freedoms gradually vanished, and moral fiber weakened. As we know, Rome eventually fell to the barbarians, and the end of a great era had arrived.

THE MIDDLE AGES. In the period known as the Middle Ages, the same social system with minor variations existed. The ruling class had its own pattern of leisure and pretty well decided what the masses, villagers and peasants, would be allowed to do. Whereas the knights did their jousting at tourneys and the gentlemen engaged in hunting and hawking, fencing, dancing, gaming, and other such activities, the common folk had their fairs, drama, celebrations, and festivals. Recreations were often carried to excess, and such activities were typically frowned upon by the third social class, the Church.

The Church glorified asceticism and hard labor. Leisure activities were generally condemned, as they tended to destroy godliness; the Spirit was to control the flesh and keep it from vices. Thus, any types of recreation gratifying the bodily senses were to be put aside because of the resulting harm to the individual seeking salvation. A total of eight weeks was typically set aside for a multitude of religious celebrations. These periods were specifically designed for purposes other than leisure pastimes. Such restrictions were difficult to enforce, however, no matter how many rules and regulations the Church laid down. We should not forget that leisure was still not something you *earned*; it was the property of one particular class in society.

The Renaissance was the beginning of a most important time for modern man. There were, of course, many influences which gradually brought about the change in attitude away from the narrow, "otherworldly" atmosphere which existed prior to the Renaissance. Intellectual advancement of a scientific nature had been taking place among non-Christians, and the Christian world finally began to realize this in the late fourteenth and fifteenth centuries. A number of humanists of this time made a strong effort to renew the earlier concept of a sound mind in a sound body—a concept that still remains only an ideal in the twentieth century. Vast economic changes were also occurring, as commerce developed throughout the known world. The rise of free cities, the developing spirit of nationalism, and the growth of industry and banking all contributed to a new way of life.

The real meaning of the Renaissance and the centuries immediately following may well be found in the spirit of inquiry which developed—a type of scientific inquiry which swept aside dogmas. The founding of many universities contributed greatly to this spread of knowledge and learning, as did the development of paper and the printing press. The power of the Church declined somewhat, as attention shifted to the problems of man attempting to carve out a good life on earth.

One may well ask why it took so long—that is, so many hundreds of years—before the possibility of earning and using leisure became a reality for the average man. This is not a simple question to answer. For one thing, there have been many wars, and these automatically destroy the surplus economy that is absolutely necessary for a high standard of education and leisure. Secondly, the traditions and mores of a civilization change slowly and probably only under concerted intellectual, social, political, and economic pressure. It took revolutions to overthrow absolutist regimes before the concept of political democracy had an opportunity to grow. Third, the almost absolute power of the Church over all aspects of men's lives had to be weakened before the concept of separation of Church and State could become a reality. Fourth, the beginnings of the natural sciences had to be consolidated into very real gains before the advanced technology could lead men into an Industrial Revolution, the total outcome of which we still cannot foresee.

Not the least of these changes was the rebirth of naturalism during the early days of the Renaissance. Actually, unrefined naturalism has been considered by some to be the oldest philosophy in the Western world, dating back to circa five hundred years before Christ. Thales, who lived in Miletus in Asia Minor, believed that he had found the final stuff of the universe within nature. He and his contemporaries saw an order in nature that was both logical and exemplary for man to follow. Both their intuition and their reason told them that man should allow nature to take its course. Here was a philosophy which had a close relationship to the individual humanism of the twelfth and thirteenth centuries. The educational aim was the development of the individual personality through a liberal education, with the "humanities" replacing the "divinities." The world of nature should be studied; the real life of the past should be examined; and the joys of living should be extolled. Physical education and sport were considered to be natural activities for man and should be encouraged. Naturalism emerged in the eighteenth century as a full-blown philosophy of life with obvious educational implications. These implications were expressed magnificently by Jean Jacques Rousseau who encouraged educators to study the child carefully and then to devise an educational plan based on this examination. The results of this approach became evident in the educational innovations of the next two centuries both in Europe and North America, not to mention certain other regions of the world. For the first time, play was recognized as a factor of considerable importance in the development of the child. The aftermath of these new ideas has been of untold value to health, physical education, and recreation.

North America

Before leisure could be used in North America, it had to be earned. Furthermore, certain prevailing ideas about idleness had to be broken down. Neither of these occurrences took place overnight. Recreational patterns have gradually emerged as the United States and Canada have grown and prospered. Initially, people originated their own recreational pursuits in an unorganized fashion. Following this, all types of commercial recreational opportunities were made available, some of dubious value. And, finally, public and voluntary agencies were created to meet the recreational needs and interests of the populace. These patterns of recreation are now proceeding concurrently in the twentieth century, and careful analysis is most difficult.

From an economic standpoint we now find ourselves in a very favorable situation, as the average work week has been cut almost in half. Many people are now choosing leisure instead of more work, because they want to "enjoy life." Many others are being forced to accept an increased amount of leisure, although they do not have all the material possessions of life that they might wish to have.

From a historical standpoint, the Puritans equated play with idleness, and hence evil, and tried to suppress it by legislation. At the same time the Virginians were enjoying a variety of recreational pursuits with relatively few twinges of conscience. The eighteenth century saw a marked change in recreational habits as some leisure was earned. Such activities as dancing, hunting, horse racing, barn raisings, and all sorts of community enterprises characterized this period. After 1800 a transitional period set in, as sectionalism caused many different patterns of recreation to flourish. The movement toward urbanization gave commercialized recreation the opportunity to develop unrestrained; yet, we might say that recreation as an organized structure of the democratic way of life was only in its infancy in the late nineteenth century.

The twentieth century has been characterized by the greatest surplus economy the world has ever seen. We have witnessed a vast new development that may be called an organized recreation pattern. The outlines of this pattern had been barely discernible toward the end of the nineteenth century, but in the past fifty years the development of public and voluntary agency recreation has been absolutely phenomenal. Further social and economic changes have taken place; professional associations have developed; professional preparation for recreational leadership has mushroomed; and city-supported recreation programs along with community centers in schools form a network across the United States and Canada.

PHILOSOPHICAL ANALYSIS

We face the final third of the twentieth century with a good deal of apprehension. Behind us are all sorts of wars, depressions, and examples of man's inhumanity to man, as well as much that gives us hope for the future. We are in the middle of a Cold War which could spell utter devastation for mankind, and yet we look ahead idealistically, realistically, pragmatically, existentially, materialistically, or what-have-you. On the home front we seek to control the tides of the business cycle. We try to comprehend the "peaceful" and the shooting revolutions going on all about us. We hear that automation may bring about a situation where people will be paid not to work. Education for leisure would seem to warrant serious consideration in the face of such a development.

History shows that no civilization has survived for long when the people had too much free time. Can we continue our unprecedented development as a continent where most people will find happiness and satisfaction despite the fact that we are increasingly crowding people together in heavily populated cities and suburbs? To answer these questions in relation to the use of leisure, we should examine our philosophical positions with their implications for education. What we decide as professionals, and what laymen will accept, will exert a considerable influence on the place of health, physical education, and recreation in our educational systems and, subsequently, in our communities at large for our mature citizens.

The *experimentalist,* the man who believes that it is only possible to find out if something is worthwhile through experience, does not like the "fractionation" that is taking place within our field, so he would immediately protest against discussing recreation education separately. For him education for the worthy use of leisure is basic to the curriculum of the school— a curriculum in which pupil growth, as defined by the experimentalist, is all-important. Secondly, play should foster moral growth, and thirdly, over-organized sport competition is not true recreation, since the welfare of the individual is often relegated to second place. The experimentalist makes it quite clear that it is a mistake to confuse the psychological distinction between work and play with the traditional economic distinction. All citizens should have ample opportunity to use their free time in a creative and fruitful manner. He would not condemn a person who watched others perform with a high level of skill in any of our cultural activities, including sport, so long as the individual kept the spectator role in the proper place. Furthermore, he would view with favor a carefully planned program of inter-scholastic sports (athletics) that is built on a sound physical education and intramural athletic base.

The *reconstructionist* believes that reality is evolving and that there is no such thing as a pre-established order in the world. Thus a fixed or universal curriculum in physical, health, and recreation education is unthinkable. His curriculum would be developed through the employment of shared planning to determine what specific contributions our field might make to the program of general education and to man's use of leisure. If the "community school concept" were employed, the student could well be offered about an hour and a half a day for recreation and relaxation alone. "Carryover" games and sports with opportunities for wholesome educational play would undoubtedly contribute to total fitness. The reconstructionist's goal is *social self-realization*; hence, creative artistic expression through recreational activities such as rhythms and dance should be emphasized. Intramural sports, compared to interscholastic athletics, rank high. Democratic method should be used to aid the group to fulfill goals—goals which themselves are the result of democratic consensus. Self-expression is important for human development, and sound recreational use of leisure would promote this particular goal.

The *realist,* the man who accepts the world at face value and who believes our experiencing it changes it not one whit, sharply differentiates work and play. Play serves a most useful purpose at recess or after school, but it should *not* be part of the regular curriculum. He would agree that the use of leisure is significant to the development of our culture, but he would also be quick to point out that "winning the Cold War" is going to take a lot more hard work and somewhat less leisure. He sees leisure pursuits or experience as an opportunity to get relief from work while it serves a re-creative purpose in the life of man. The surplus energy theory of play and recreation makes sense to him. So does the more recent bio-social theory of play—the idea that play helps the organism to achieve balance. He would tend to deprecate the fact that the "play attitude" seems to be missing almost completely in many organized sports. Play (and recreation) is, therefore, very important to the realist; it should be "liberating" with people developing their potentialities for wholesome hobbies through recreation. As he sees it, recreation can serve as a "safety valve" for the reduction of life's psychic tensions. Even though play should not be considered as a basic part of the curriculum, we should not forget that it provides an "indispensable seasoning" to the good life. Extracurricular play and recreational activities and a sound general education should suffice to equip the student for leisure activities in our society.

The *idealist,* having both a firm belief in an intrinsic system of educational values and an extreme concern with individual personality and its development, is ambiguous about the role of recreation in the school and in adult life. It is the duty of the idealist, therefore, to reassess the contributions that recreation and play can and do make in the education of man—education as he defines it.

Another difficulty that confronts idealists is deciding on the roles of physical education and recreation. Perhaps only *physical* education should be included in the educational hierarchy, and all other recreational needs should be met by the recreation administrator (either within the school system or in the community). On the other hand, an idealist might view favorably a theory of recreation and play which grants educational possibilities to these activities of man. The self-expression theory of play suggests that man's chief need in life is to be able to give expression to his own personality—a theory obviously quite compatible with the conception of man as an organic unity. Idealists believe that man is a purposive being who is striving to achieve those values which are embedded in reality itself. To the extent that the idealist can realize the eternal values through the choice of the right kinds of play and recreation without flouting the moral order in the world, he will be progressive enough to disregard a dualistic theory of work and play—a theory that has plagued us in North America down to the present day.

There are distinct signs that specific Protestant denominations are becoming increasingly aware of the role that recreation can play in the promulgation of the Christian idealistic way of life. In the United States such recognition has been largely a twentieth-century phenomenon. Recreation has developed to the point where it is now clearly one of the major social institutions in American life. If "the ideal suggests the integrated individual in an integrated society growing in the image of the integrated universe," then all types of recreational experience and activity can seemingly make a contribution to the realization of this "ideal." We are warned that mankind is faced with a "recreational imperative."

Existentialistic thought gives play an important place. Personal liberation is highly desirable, and this is most certainly a function of play. In sporting activities the individual can be free as he selects his own values and achieves self-expression. The child can create his own world of play and thereby realize his true identity. Obviously, varsity athletics, as typically conducted, would be almost completely antithetical to the existentialist. The existentialist at play wants no prescribed formations, no coach calling the plays and destroying the player's "authenticity," and no crowd exhorting him to win at any cost. A perfect example of the use of *language analysis* to help man better understand the use of his leisure in sport and athletics is provided by James Keating (1964, p. 28).

section five

AMATEUR,
SEMIPROFESSIONAL, AND
PROFESSIONAL ATHLETICS

The relationship of these three areas to one another, to the educational system, and to the entire culture must be more fully understood. This brief treatment should help the physical, health, and recreation education teacher to comprehend the issues at stake. Sport (a pleasurable diversion) and athletics (a highly competitive activity) are both parts of the very life-blood of our field and offer the possibility of great benefits and satisfaction to the participant and coach alike. They are significant cultural influences which offer the possibility of good or bad to the society. Thus we should ask ourselves, In what way may sport and athletics be used for the service of man?

People engage in games and sport today for many reasons. Psychologists have revealed some of the complexities of determining motivation. Do people really know why they do a particular thing, or are they suppressing their reasons? Or have these reasons been "determined" for them by their home and social environments? Keeping these reservations in mind, we ask: Do we take part in games and sport for fun, for re-creation, for self-expression, for health, for exercise, for competition, or perhaps because of the money or other benefits it might bring us? Or do we do it for a variety of reasons, some stronger at times than others? Or perhaps we have never even given it any thought at all!

HISTORICAL BACKGROUND

Primitive and preliterate man undoubtedly felt the urge to play; so, he did. Often he took part in games as part of his religious observances. And there is no denying that sport served a very practical purpose as well. It gave him the opportunity to practice skills upon which he relied for his very survival.

The urge to play is probably older than any so-called human culture since animals play in the same ways that men do. It has been stated that civilization has contributed no significant aspect to the general concept of play, although we must admit that considerable thought and investigation has been devoted to the matter. It is possible that scientific investigation will eventually give us the answer to the question, or perhaps we may never really know the reason. Did God give man a play instinct, or did nature give us play—play whose very essence defies all analysis; play which appears to be completely irrational; play which is both beautiful and ridiculous at one and the same time. It is free and voluntary and seemingly not concerned with the serious business of life. Yet it can be and often is completely absorbing; it starts and stops at a given moment; and it has rules.

It is the so-called "higher forms" of play with which we will concern ourselves primarily, and especially those types which eventually became semi-professional and professional in the Graeco-Roman period. But before we come to this phase of the development, we should consider briefly the early relationship of sport to religious observances. Here we find the early idea that play is dedicated to the deity. The ritual or performance is played or "represented" in a designated area. It may be a sacrifice, a performance, or a contest. The hope is that the gods will observe the sacred contest and give their approval by causing the event to actually take place. Such a contest might be between the hero of the particular culture involved and some arch foe who is vanquished by superior skill, wile, or good fortune.

A great many of the primitive games obviously served an extremely useful purpose. Contests involving the use of a club, a spear, and a bow and arrow developed proficiency in the use of weapons. Other activities such as wrestling, fighting, running, horse racing, and swimming were also highly useful activities in life and the struggle for survival, and these sports today are "vestigial remains" of earlier civilizations. These games demanded in most instances such attributes as strength, endurance, skill and dexterity of movement, as well as "control of the passions." Thus inclusion of this vigorous play activity would seem to be warranted in all educational systems in some form or another.

Similar sports and recreation were part of life to a greater or lesser degree in all of the early civilizations. Egyptians took part in all sorts of gymnastic exercises and field sports. This was especially true for the nobility and for those whose profession was arms, but the masses had their games and amusements as well. In Babylonia and Assyria the skills of hunting and fighting were shown preference, and there are many passages in the Bible that refer to the physical activities of the Hebrews. However, Israel could not be called a "sporting nation" in any sense of the word.

The early aristocrats in China were active sportsmen. The contests in swordsmanship brought this skill to a high level, and wrestling, jiu-jitsu, and boxing were very popular during particular eras, as were butting and football, the latter a game in which a round ball was kicked within a prescribed area. Even the games of polo and golf may trace their origins to ancient China. In India, boxing, wrestling, and hunting were popular activities for warriors. And in Iran, a nation in which the warrior was very prominent, most of the accepted sports had a close relationship to the arts of war, with the possible exception of polo. This latter activity was extremely popular for a considerable period of time, and the Persians became very skillful at it.

The Cretan and Mycenaean warriors engaged in similar warlike sports around the sixteenth century B.C. Hunting, for example, was a favorite of these people. The art of bull-grappling was an unusual sport of the Minoan Age. Strangely enough, both men and women practiced this dangerous sport. The activity was evidently connected with religious observance. Other sports included boxing, wrestling, hunting, and fishing, as well as acrobatic dancing by both sexes.

Greece

Although Spartans went to the extreme in the physical training of both their men and women, the Spartan government was actually against extreme specialization in athletics. They did compete very successfully, however, in wrestling, boxing, jumping, running, and throwing of the javelin and discus in the early Olympics. Boxing and the pancratium were activities in which the Spartans were not allowed to enter in the various sacred games, but there appears to be evidence that they were encouraged at home. Hunting was extremely popular in this warlike nation. Ball playing was also a favorite activity of Spartan youth.

In Athens, young men spent a great deal of time in the palaestra being trained by a man known as a paidotribe. This specialist was responsible for general physical development of youth, while the gymnast was more of an expert in specific athletic contests. The paidotribe trained boys from the age of seven to about fifteen in a variety of activities, and, in many instances, parents selected this instructor with great care. Concern was expressed, however, about early overspecialization in preparation for subsequent participation in the Games. Eventually boys graduated from the palaestra, and the sons of the wealthy went to the gymnasium for further training in sport. Some talented boys were selected for further instruction even though they came from poorer families—possibly the first athletic scholarships! But they did find difficulty in taking sufficient time away from their daily work.

Training in the gymnasium was much more vigorous, and the aim was a much higher degree of perfection. Here we see the appearance of the first "wealthy alumnus" who assumed the role of a sort of graduate manager of athletics. He was known as the gymnasiarch, and it was he who directed the gymnasium and the various festivals. Some of these gymnasiums were really elaborate structures with many rooms and facilities. Again we find a close connection between sport and religion; in each gymnasium there was a shrine where a particular deity was worshipped. The fact that there were public gymnasiums also indicates the responsibility that the city-state felt for the physical training of its youth. A system of "ephebic" training was subsequently instituted to bring to a climax the preparation of the warrior-citizen between the ages of eighteen and twenty.

From time to time, games and sport succeeded in unifying the city-states of Greece, where nothing else, not even religion, could. Of course, it has been said that the real religion of the Greeks was their concern for beauty, strength, and health. The need for the highest type of physical skill and conditioning was quite understandable, as they were involved almost constantly in one type of struggle or another. Sparta achieved early distinction through military triumphs, made possible largely through training in sport. The Athenians recognized this and pursued athletics most vigorously especially when the city-state's freedom was endangered. The Hellenic ideal was to meet life head-on and to win.

There were all sorts of games and festivals conducted at the various levels of the society. Private sporting contests led to local games. Then there were contests within the different city-states for representatives from the various communities. These games were expanded still further into regional events such as the quadrennial Panathenaic games established in 566 B.C. The greatest contests, of course, were the Panhellenic games—the most famous of these being the Olympic Games held first at Olympia in 776 B.C. These contests were so important that a sort of "international truce" was declared for the period before, during, and after the Games.

Elimination contests in all events were held throughout the land prior to the Games, with only freeborn Greeks allowed to compete. Upon their arrival at Olympia athletes were carefully examined and took the Olympic oath promising to obey all the rules which were established. Great dishonor and shame was the fate of the athlete who cheated or otherwise broke the strict rules; hence such infractions were rare. Approximately 45,000 spectators filled the stadium and held their places day in and day out over the five-day period despite miserable sanitary conditions. The pentathlon was a most important event that included the broad jump, the discus throw, the spear throw, the stadium sprint, and wrestling. The victor had to score first in three of the five events. Other events included boxing, the pancratium, various running races, horse races, and chariot races.

The winner of an event received a laurel wreath—a "crown" of wild olives placed on top of a woolen fillet wound around the head. Soon all sorts of prizes were awarded including vases and oil from the sacred olives which was dispensed in amphorae (vase-like containers with handles). First prize was usually worth five times as much as second, and the "youth" classification winners received slightly higher awards than those in the "boys" group. For example, the winner of the pentathlon for boys received 30 amphorae of olive oil, while second place was awarded six. But the winner of the pentathlon for youth earned 40 amphorae, and the second-place contestant received eight amphorae of olive oil. The winner of the chariot race with full-grown horses was awarded 140 amphorae, possibly because this event was more expensive to the participants. Such awards did not exceed contestants' expenses at any rate, so soon there were more semiprofessional boxers and wrestlers than horse and chariot racers.

There did appear to be a relationship between politics and athletics as political decline set in. After the Peloponnesian War, Athens had many economic problems. The Macedonians with their professional soldiers and improved methods of warfare sealed the fate of the amateur citizen-soldier at Chaeronaea in 338 B.C. After that, the former social ideal was never regained, as Athens' sphere of control continued to decline. There developed an intellectualism and a decline in physical fitness as mercenaries took over the defense of the city-state. And as amateur athletics lost influence, professional athletics gained stature. There had been, of course, many indirect rewards for the earlier winners at the Olympic Games, but this was a far cry from the subsequent professionalism.

But even in the earlier days overspecialization in sport occasioned by the desire to win had tended to tarnish the luster of the so-called amateur ideal. The very nature of sport made it difficult to judge, and the goal of excellence in a number of sports as part of overall harmony seemed to be an unattainable objective. If a man wanted to win, he specialized. The more he specialized, the more time he spent in one particular phase of sport, and the less he had for other aspects of his cultural development and for his livelihood. If he were wealthy enough, of course, at least he didn't have to worry about where his next meal was coming from—often a serious concern for our "amateur" athletes today in certain "non-gate-receipt" sports!

Extreme specialization in a particular sport often resulted in distorted musculature. Combative sports tended to have a brutalizing effect on the participants, who, in many cases, were disfigured in various ways. Their habits of eating, sleeping, and living in general became specialized. Specialized trainers and coaches arose and the athletes whom they trained achieved pre-eminence. As athletics became a career for a certain group of men, it was obvious that the former "amateur" athlete would be foolish to engage in any contest with a professional. The ideal of amateurism survived for a time at Olympia, where the rule of amateurism was rigidly enforced, but the maintenance of such a standard became increasingly difficult. Cities began to compete for the services of the better performers, and the worst type of professionalism soon became a reality. Materialistic influence won out over the earlier idealism of a social ideal; such were the characteristics of sport in an age of decline of the great city-state.

Athletics became a business, and athletes themselves were often exploited in the worst sort of way. The result was that soon various athletic guilds and associations were formed to protect the rights of athletes and to secure them greater benefits. By the middle of the third century A.D., successful athletes regularly applied for and were granted pensions for life under Roman law. But despite all these "advances," which were considerable from a materialistic standpoint, social influences eventually brought about the downfall of the professional athlete. Rome became increasingly decadent and was crumbling before the attacks of its enemies. Christianity condemned the morals of the Empire, and, in a matter of time, the Roman government officially adopted the Christian religion. The 291st Olympiad appears to have marked the last celebration of the Olympic Games, abolished by Theodosius the Great in 393 A.D. This signalled the death knell of what had become professional sport in the Graeco-Roman world.

ROME. During the seventh and sixth centuries B.C., the Latins invaded Etrurian territory and founded Rome. Etruscans had related sport to religious rituals; their annual games were extremely important to them. But when the active Romans began their own conquests, they used sports to help them achieve efficiency at arms. Later, when the military went professional, games and sport were relied on to maintain health and to give personal pleasure and group entertainment. Thus the significance of games change from a religious function (to gain the gods' favor for various ventures) to a purely hedonistic one.

the middle ages

Sport and athletics in the Middle Ages presented a most dismal picture according to present standards. Asceticism and scholasticism dominated the society of Europe generally, and the physical pleasures that might arise for the masses from participation in recreational sports were frowned upon in official quarters. For example, some amusements evidently interfered with archery practice by nobles and were banned, as was "weight-putting" by Edward III. These ordinances were very difficult to enforce especially during the time of fairs, celebrations, and festivals.

After the Norman Conquest of England in 1066, the ruling class developed its own pattern of leisure, which included jousting at tourneys. Gentlemen engaged in hunting, hawking, fencing, archery, and other war-related activities. The historians of the time made only occasional references to purely recreational pursuits. A barren intellectual and philosophical life dominated by Christian dogmatism, along with tribe-like political conditions and rude manners and customs, did much to suppress creativity, aesthetic expression, and sporting activity of even a fairly high type.

During the Renaissance and the Reformation the attitude toward participation in sport was gradually changing. In England, for example, during the reign of Henry VIII (1509–1547), there is evidence of a resurgence of interest in athletics. He himself liked to throw the hammer. There were those, however, who were against games and sport for scholars. Roger Ascham opposed athletic activity, while Sir Thomas Elyot felt that accomplishment in sport was highly desirable in light of extreme study conditions and flogging. James I and subsequent Stuart kings supported the idea of sporting contests for the development of manliness in their offspring. An annual football match was extremely popular in Chester during the fifteenth century, but was supplanted by various running races after 1500. During the Puritan rule and that of Charles II to 1685, interest in athletics dropped off very sharply. We need hardly add that this discussion has been confined to a consideration of the activities of the sons of the upper class. The average man needed leisure before games and sport could truly become an important part of his life.

THE UNITED STATES

We will now transfer our attention almost exclusively to a brief treatment of the history of sport in American life. The focus will be narrowed, and fairly sharply, to a consideration of what may properly be called amateur sport, semiprofessional sport, and professional sport. Our concern for the status of school and college athletics throughout the discussion will be readily apparent.

The distinctly different attitudes of the Puritans and the Virginians toward recreational pursuits has already been mentioned. With the easing off of living conditions during the eighteenth century, a certain amount of leisure was earned. Such activities as dancing, hunting, horse racing, barn raisings, wrestling, and a variety of so-called community enterprises characterized this period. Life began to change considerably in the United States after the Revolutionary War as a new spirit of nationalism began to make itself felt. The need for physical training as preparation for military fitness was apparent to many at this time, but the significance of play, and the possible inclusion of it along with physical training in the educational curriculum, was not comprehended. The national history of the United States ran parallel with the history of the academies—schools for boys which aimed to prepare youth to meet life and its many problems. With the great job of carving out the West ahead it was not long before practical education won out and increased consideration was being given to the physical welfare of the student.

By the end of the first quarter of the nineteenth century, great changes were taking place in the lives of the people due to increasing industrialization and urbanization. The new way of life eliminated many of the former vigorous activities that characterized life on an expanding frontier. Leisure patterns were changing: There was considerable commercial entertainment and not too much opportunity for active participation because of lack of play space. There were many, of course, who still had to work long hours for their livelihood. The games and sporting tradition was basically that of England with its two-class society, so it was logical that we should inherit the English concept of amateurism. Some sports quite naturally seemed more appropriate for well-to-do individuals who were able to afford their own social and athletic clubs.

Interest in a variety of sports increased in the first half of the nineteenth century. Bowling and swimming became popular activities, as did rowing and cricket. Cricket was to be eventually supplanted by baseball, which, despite its strong relationship to "rounders," was considered an indigenous American sport. The first intercollegiate baseball game is reported to have been played by Williams and Amherst in 1859. Origins of American football date back at least as far as an intramural contest played at Harvard in 1827, although there is earlier evidence of a sort of football game being played on the New Haven green in 1807. Concurrently, German gymnastics achieved brief popularity around Boston in the early part of the century.

It wasn't until after the Civil War that interest in athletic sports really began to grow. The war showed very definitely that there was a need for physical training of America's young men. The American Gymnastic Union (Turners) promoted the introduction of German gymnastics in our public schools vigorously and successfully. Innumerable athletic leagues, both amateur and professional, were formed, and college and university students promoted such activities despite considerable opposition from faculty and administration.

Rowing, baseball, and football were the first intercollegiate sports to be organized to any extent, although track and field should probably be included in this listing as well. The first intercollegiate rowing race was between Yale and Harvard in 1852; the first baseball game, between Amherst and Williams in 1859; the first football game, between Princeton and Rutgers in 1869; and the first intercollegiate track and field meet was an Ivy League affair in 1874 with Harvard, Yale, Princeton, Columbia, and Cornell participating.

After 1870, intercollegiate athletics grew so rapidly, and so many problems developed, that college and university administrators and faculty realized that something had to be done; sport had to be made to conform to certain acceptable standards, or it had to be eliminated. Intercollegiate football was especially troublesome because of a disproportionate number of injuries and flagrant practices. In 1905, representatives of about thirty institutions held a meeting which resulted in the formation of the Intercollegiate Athletic Association of the United States. (The name was later changed to the National Collegiate Athletic Association.) This organization has done all in its power to promote sound intercollegiate athletic programs; from the outset, though, it was urged that individual institutions assume responsibility for high standards of conduct in the administration of interscholastic athletic competition. Obviously, this has been a most difficult goal to achieve.

Another extremely important organization in the history of athletics in the United States, and throughout the world for that matter, has been the Amateur Athletic Union of the United States. This group was formed by interested sportsmen in 1888 to remedy a serious situation in nonschool and college athletics, controlled at that time by undesirable individual promoters. The A.A.U. has accepted the traditional British viewpoint that "an amateur athlete is one who engages in sports for the pleasure and physical, mental, or social benefits he derives therefrom and to whom sport is nothing more than an avocation." The promulgation of this ideal has persisted to the present day. In addition, the A.A.U. was instrumental in reviving the Olympic Games in 1896. In the United States, the country was divided into a number of districts with all the athletic clubs within a district forming an association that had representation at the national level. There gradually developed a number of allied sports-governing bodies in certain sports over which the A.A.U. does not have full jurisdiction.

While all this was taking place, certain early twentieth-century educators were stressing the value of play in the total educative process. This had a marked effect on the secondary schools whose enrollments had been increasing sharply. School playgrounds were being developed, and the popular literature of the time stressed that participation in sport tended to improve young people's attitudes toward desirable group behavior and citizenship. Thus, sports and games gradually began to rival gymnastic instruction in the school program. A survey conducted on a national level in 1905 showed that the majority of superintendents of public school systems approved of including interscholastic athletics in the school program. There were opponents and those who gave half-hearted approval, however, and it was stressed that such athletic competition had to be regulated carefully and should not be overemphasized because it served the needs and interests of only relatively few students.

Thus high school athletics began at the end of the nineteenth century and during the early years of the twentieth century. There was a pattern to follow—that of the colleges and universities. Such a pattern was a help, but it did bring about overemphasis that many claim has never been corrected. As on the college level, leagues that standardized regulations for control of interschool competition were formed. Eventually state-wide athletic associations were needed, and the final phase took place in 1920 with the organization of the National Federation of State High School Athletic Associations. Down through the years many difficult problems have been faced and overcome through the dedication of interested educators, but the matter of overemphasis plagues us even today.

Another interesting trend has been the rise of intramural sport competition at the college level, and to a certain extent at other educational levels. Sociological influences such as wars and depressions have influenced sport and physical recreational development appreciably. World War I, for example, brought about almost universal physical education legislation in the U.S., making possible the introduction of sports skill programs into what had been formerly "physical training" periods. So it was that physical education periods in the schools, with California taking the lead, changed to sessions where sport rather than gymnastics dominated in the years between the end of the war and the early 1930s.

The decade from 1920 to 1930 was an interesting one in many ways, and the growth that took place in sport participation was no exception. Tremendous spectator interest in many high school, college, and professional sports developed. There was a demand for huge athletic stadia, which, once constructed, had to be filled. Athletic coaches and playground leaders were desperately needed, and the number of professional preparation programs increased sharply. During this period the N.C.A.A. emphasized the need for faculty control of athletics rather than administration by students and alumni. Conference formation and the elimination of seasonal coaches had been stressed during the previous decade. Thus, concern in the 1920s was more a matter of the standardization of rules for the various sports and the development of programs for championships at the national level. The seemingly ever-present problem of subsidization and recruitment was so bad that several groups, including the N.C.A.A., requested a survey by the Carnegie Foundation in 1926. The report, entitled *American College Athletics,* was published in 1929 and contained a serious indictment of practices in men's intercollegiate sports. There was no question but that semiprofessionalism had arrived in American college sport.

Also during this period the Olympic Games program was enlarged to include many more sports, a greater number of participants, and competition for women. The classic definition of an amateur as accepted by the A.A.U. many years before continued, although times and conditions had changed; it became a matter of principle—a principle which, according to the A.A.U., was the only means by which the United States could be represented honorably in the quadrennial Games. The decision regarding the amateur status of the participants from a particular country rested solely with the country that was certifying its own athletes as amateurs. What others did under the guise of amateurism was not our concern; what we did was our own problem, and how we did it will make a most interesting study for future sports historians!

The period since 1930 in the United States has been one in which interest in competitive sport and physical recreation has continued unabated, and has, in fact, grown. The use of leisure has become an urgent concern. High school athletics have attained new heights, as have college athletics and international competition. Competition in sport has helped to promote a concept of internationalism. But who can deny the undercurrents of nationalism present in the Cold War athletic contests between the U.S. and the U.S.S.R.? Furthermore, behind the scenes, the gnawing, persistent problem of amateurism has plagued us and made a mockery of the high ideals for which we strive. The words of that cynic haunt us: "Amateurs? There ain't none!"

And so in the 1960s the United States finds itself the scene of a titanic struggle between the Amateur Athletic Union and the National Collegiate Athletic Association for control of what is still called "amateur sport," although an attempt by anyone to offer a blanket definition of that is an absolute impossibility. A dictionary, of course, goes along with the norm, explaining an amateur as one not rated as a professional, and a professional as a person who has competed in sport for a stake or purse, or gate money, or with a professional for a prize, or who has taught or trained in sports or athletics for pay. Which brings us back to that cynic, who says, "An amateur is a guy who won't take a check!"

Some one group is going to win this struggle, but not before the United States is terribly embarrassed or before many fine young athletes are hurt in one way or another. What appears to be needed is some frank, straightforward thinking which takes into consideration that the United States has entered the second half of the twentieth century, and that history may seem to be repeating itself *but not in the same way.* As often as this theme has been reiterated: Your outlook on this problem will depend a great deal on your philosophy of education.

PHILOSOPHICAL ANALYSIS

The *essentialist* will tend to believe that the classic definition of amateurism has considerable merit. He will be apt to wish to retain the good from the past and to change the status quo very slowly if at all. If, for example, it can be proved scientifically that a change is needed, certain people holding philosophical positions within educational essentialism would be willing to accept change. Others are skeptical about so-called "scientific proof" in certain areas of human life; rather, they believe that "right is right, and wrong is wrong."

The *progressivist* believes that there are no values that are absolutely fixed and that changing times demand new methods. He appreciates the contributions of the past, but doesn't regard them as sacrosanct. He would be willing to accept a new approach to this perennial problem in sport if it worked; his attitude is that we can only arrive at a solution to this problem by trying out some of the proposed solutions on a trial and error basis.

The *experimentalist* believes that physical education classes and intramural sports are more important to the large majority of students than interscholastic and intercollegiate sports and deserve priority if conflict arises over budgetary allotment, staff allotment, or use of facilities. He can give full support to team experiences in competitive sports, because they can be vital educational experiences if properly conducted. He believes further that "physical" educational, athletic, or "physical" recreational activity at a reasonable level of skill can be an aesthetic experience of a fine type. If stress is placed on the continuous development of standards to guide conduct, a significant contribution may be made to moral training through laboratory experiences. Thus, the planned occurrence of educational situations within sports competition is important to the experimentalist.

The *reconstructionist* would stress intramural sports and voluntary physical recreational activities. In team competition particular stress should be placed on cooperation and the promotion of *friendly* competition. Extramural athletic competition can be introduced when there is a need, inasmuch as striving for excellence is important in individual development, but this aspect of the program must be kept in balance with the total curriculum. Educators must zealously guard against the exploitation evident in many interscholastic and intercollegiate competitive athletic programs. Sport was created *for* man, and we cannot permit materialistic influences in our society to "win out" over sound educational philosophy. Instruction in carry-over games and sports (the whole concept of education for leisure) should have an important place in the curriculum.

The *realist* is typically concerned with the adequate training and development of the body itself. He gives "qualified approval" to competitive sport, because he believes that it contributes to the learning of sportsmanship and desirable social conduct. Some realists might agree that every child should be *required* to learn a team game and an individual sport that could be played as an adult before graduation. Competitive athletics, however, are extracurricular and should come after the official school day is over. The underlying reasoning, therefore, is that work and play cannot be identified under the same psychological rubric. Play for young adults is "carefree activity performed for its own sake" and for the sake of re-creation. Unfortunately, this "play attitude" is quite often missing from organized sport.

The *idealist* definitely favors sport and athletics in our culture; after all, witness the status accorded such activity in ancient Greek idealism. He believes in the transfer of training theory which implies that attitudes of sportsmanship and fair play learned through desirable athletic competition can and do transfer to life situations. The Christian idealist believes that a coach should fulfill the moral and ethical demands of his calling by setting a good example for his charges to emulate; the athlete, therefore, should strive "for that same perfection that we seek on our athletic teams" in his individual life. The desired moral and social values that sport can yield must be made realities. The teacher of sports is actually in a unique position, because he can be one of the most influential members of the school community in the shaping of these values. But he must be careful not to let his boys become too self-centered; sport should be a means to an end, not an end in itself. Extreme specialization may warp the personalities of all concerned. As Oberteuffer has emphasized time and again, we cannot be satisfied with scores instead of character.

The *existentialist* challenges the profession by asking, How is it possible to preserve the individual's authenticity in individual, dual, and team sports where winning is so often overemphasized? In true sport, as opposed to competitive athletics, a young man may personally select the values he wishes to derive from activity. Man should play, therefore, for actualization of self and *should use sport for his own purposes.* In this way he will find personal liberation and release.

CONCLUSION. This brief summary of the background of sport and competitive athletics in the Western world, has indicated that athletic competition is accepted to a greater or lesser degree as an integral or ancillary phase of the educative process. *No one can deny that vigorous competitive sport has become a vital phase of our American way of life!* A great many of us are coaches of one or more sports at the different levels of public education, and there is no question but that we can make our influence felt as to the direction that we believe athletic competition should take in the future. Such influence as we may have in the future determination of policy will achieve results only as we are articulate, logical, and consistent in the arguments we present to our "academic" colleagues, who are often not quite convinced of the worth of our enterprise: Hence our task is to make a case for athletics based on a carefully conceived philosophy of education. In the past we have tended instead to rely on the great interest which competitive sport generates in the student population and in the community-at-large.

What influence we can have at the conference level, at the district and national level in the various sports-governing bodies, and at the international level depends largely upon the degree of "enlightened participation" we are willing to assume whenever and wherever the opportunity presents itself. The truly professional person, who is dedicated to the promotion of the highest and finest type of sport competition, cannot be satisfied just with doing his own work; he must fight off any lethargy "to let George do it" in the professional associations and the sports-governing bodies where the policies for the future are being formulated. The average coach feels that he, as merely one individual, doesn't have much to say about this problem of the amateur, semiprofessional, and professional in sport. He fails to realize that united with other like-minded coaches in, for example, the Men's Athletic Division of the American Association for Health, Physical Education, and Recreation, this Division could have a strong influence on the future of American sport. It is true that any such progress will necessarily involve cooperative effort with the N.C.A.A., the A.A.U., the National Association of Intercollegiate Athletics, the National Federation of State High School Athletic Associations, and other similar groups, but has it not been characteristic of our American democratic way of life to work things out amicably for the good of all?

It may well be that we will have to reevaluate some of our treasured assumptions about the amateur code in athletics. What *are* the reasons today for the sharp distinction between the amateur and the professional? History tells us where the ideal originated, but it also tells us that the conditions which brought it about do not exist in America today. It is quite possible that we are trying desperately to perpetuate a concept which has outserved its purpose. Must we persist in the ideology that in sport and athletics it is a question of black or white—the professional being the black one, and the amateur, the white? Can't we recognize and identify the many shades of "gray" that inevitably exist in between?

What is so wrong with a young sportsman or athlete being classified as "gray," or a semiprofessional? Do we brand the musician, the artist, or the sculptor in our society who develops his talent sufficiently to receive some remuneration for his efforts as being a "dirty pro"? Why must this idea persist in sport—a legitimate phase of our culture? The answer to these questions may well lie in the fact that we are not willing, almost subconsciously, to accept sport as a legitimate and worthwhile aspect of our culture.

The materialistic image of today's professional in sport and athletics does not help very much either. Granted he is a different breed than his predecessor, especially in such sports as basketball and football, but even here he is a "professional" in the limited sense of the word. He is usually after all the money that his physical talent can bring him on the open market. He sees professional athletics as a means to an end—his security and ultimate happiness in life. There is nothing basically wrong with using a talent in this way, but a greater societal good would result if he would attempt to make himself a professional in the broader sense of the word. Everything considered, this man has an unusual talent he has developed to a high degree in a cultural activity that has proved itself important in our society. Furthermore, it is probably true that a professional who has reached his peak attainment is better qualified in this sphere of activity than he will ever be in any other. What would be more natural than to expect this man to become a true professional and to devote the rest of his life to the promotion of his sport with the youth and adults of his country? There is absolutely no reason why the professional sportsman-athlete, a man who typically loves his sport, cannot devote his life to a social ideal and become a really fine professional individual—one whose primary aim in life is to serve his fellowman. Such an approach can work; the country is dotted with men and women who have made it work. It is not as idealistic as it may sound. It would do much to help us look at the "amateur controversy" in a new light.

We cannot agree with the cynic who says that there are no more amateurs in sport. This is not true. There are, and will always be, amateurs in the only logical sense of the word today. The amateur is the beginner, the dabbler, the dilettante. This is not saying that he "loves" the activity any more or less than the semiprofessional or professional. As a matter of fact, he isn't well enough acquainted with it to "love" it. When the businessman goes out to the local golf course early on a Sunday morning and turns in a neat score of one hundred and twenty-five for eighteen holes, he is displaying all the traits of an amateur in what should be today's parlance.

Proficiency in the chosen sport, and the amount of time spent practicing it, should certainly be considered when we classify sportsmen. The boy who plays the trumpet in the high school band is an amateur. If he qualifies to play in his college dance band on Saturday nights and receives 15 dollars weekly for his efforts, he is a semiprofessional. Who would criticize him for this? Let us assume that this young man is majoring in music and goes on after college to become either a professional musician or a professional teacher. We find this perfectly commendable in our society. But there are a great many people in the United States who can't visualize this in athletics. The first time an athlete takes 15 dollars for playing his favorite sport, he is a professional and, *presumably,* could be barred from any attempt to participate in the Olympic Games. Obviously, such a stand is ridiculous today.

It is, of course, the excesses and overemphasis that are feared. The United States is committed to a great educational experiment on a grand scale. We are the only country in the world where thirty-five to forty per cent of the young people go on to some form of higher education in the more than 2000 junior colleges, community colleges, colleges, and universities. Semiprofessionalism to a fairly high degree in college sport can possibly be justified only for physical education majors and those who might wish to become professionals in those sports which bring in fairly high gate receipts. Because winning teams in college sports bring prestige and gate receipts, competition for fine athletes is keen. The N.C.A.A. and the N.A.I.A. have made athletic scholarships legitimate with certain stipulations. Many people felt that the Western Conference (Big Ten) was only being realistic when it removed the "need factor" from its athletic tender plan; others felt this was a serious mistake. Other important colleges and universities admit students on the basis of their intellectual attainment and many other factors, of which athletic accomplishment is one. Then scholarship aid is given on the basis of the parents' total financial position—their ability to pay for their son's college education. No matter which approach is used, the athlete is still being subsidized to a greater or lesser extent. It is extremely difficult to say which approach is right and best for the individual and for society. One thing is certain: Whatever help the young man receives should be known by all and should be in conformity with established rules and regulations.

V

Progress as a Concept

Has progress in physical, health, and recreation education been made through the agency of the school and other educational agencies? This chapter will attempt to answer that question in view of a brief consideration of the concept of progress itself. We shall also discuss educational progress and its relationship to educational philosophy and conclude with a statement about the need for consensus in physical, health, and recreation education.

In the first two sections the conclusions of particular scientific and educational authorities will be presented. The writer will rely on his own subjective judgment in the third section relating to physical, health, and recreation education. Any fusion of the past and the present, which this effort undoubtedly is, cannot escape the element of controversy and struggle. Thus the writer recognizes that it is literally impossible for him to have historical perspective or to be completely unbiased.

Furthermore, the reader may find that he 1) has already made a number of judgments for himself; 2) is currently in the process of making these judgments; or 3) will make these judgments for himself once he understands the problems more fully. One's judgment could well be determined by the mood he is in or by the prevailing mood of the times. The man or woman who thinks profoundly in the light of the occurrences of the twentieth century cannot be blamed for being pessimistic or skeptical at best. If he can be classified as a pessimistic person, he will probably feel that man's future prospects on this earth are not good at all. Perhaps you are an optimist, however. At any rate, your considered philosophy—that is, you the reader as a professional person—will have much to do with your future plans and the way you go about executing them. Keep in mind also that thoughts expressed in words are just that and nothing more. Others will judge you and your efforts by your deeds as a professional person—not by what you say you believe. Hopefully, they won't prejudge you. You live your philosophy every day of your life. That is why it is so important to know where you are going and why you want to get there. It is for this reason that this particular persistent problem has been placed at the end of the book.

A DEFINITION OF PROGRESS

Any study of history inevitably forces a person to conjecture about man's progress. A world-famous paleontologist, George Gaylord Simpson, after twenty-five years of research, offers us his assessment of the concept of progress in evolution (1949, pp. 240–62). His study has convinced him that it is necessary to reject "the over-simple and metaphysical concept of a pervasive perfection principle." That there has been progression he will not deny, but is this "progress"? The difficulty comes when we assume that change is progress; man must ask himself if he can recommend a criterion by which progress may be judged.

We are warned that it may be shortsighted for man to be his own "judge and jury" in this connection. It may well be an acceptable *human* criterion of progress to say that he is coming closer to approximating what he thinks a man ought to be and to achieving what he holds to be good. It is not wise, according to Simpson, however, to automatically assume that this is "the *only* criterion of progress and that it has a *general* validity in evolution. . . ." Thus, throughout the history of life there have been examples of progress and examples of retrogression, and progress is "certainly not a basic property of life common to all its manifestations." If it is a materialistic world, as Simpson would have us believe, a particular species can progress and retrogress. There is "a tendency for life to expand, to fill in all the space in the livable environments," but such expansion has not necessarily been constant (although it is true that man is now "the most rapidly progressing organism in the world").

It is true further that man has made progress in adaptability and has developed his "ability to cope with a greater variety of environments." This is also progress considered from the human vantage point. The various evolutionary phenomena among the many species, however, do not show "a vital principle common to all forms of life," and "they are certainly inconsistent with the existence of a supernal perfecting principle. . . ." Thus, Simpson concludes, man's progress is actually relative and not general, and "does not warrant choice of the line of man's ancestry as the central line of evolution as a whole." Yet it is safe to say that "man is among the highest products of evolution . . . and that man is, on the whole but not in every single respect, the pinnacle so far of evolutionary progress" *on this earth*.

With these sobering thoughts, with the realization that evolution (of man and other organisms) is going on and will probably continue for millions of years, we can realize how futile it is to attempt to predict any outcome for the ceaseless change so evident in life and its environment. We can say that man must be extremely careful about the possible extinction of his species on earth, because it is highly improbable, though not absolutely impossible, that his development would be repeated. Some other mammal might develop in a similar way, but this will not happen so long as man has control of his environment and does not encourage such development. Man's task is to attempt to modify and perhaps to control the direction of his own evolution according to his highest goals. It may be possible through the agency of education to ensure the future of our species; one way to accomplish this would be to place a much greater emphasis on the social sciences and to work for an ethically sound world-state.

PROGRESS IN EDUCATION

Now let us transfer our attention from Professor Simpson's concept of progress in evolution to the more immediate problem of the United States at the end of the twentieth century—to the type of society we may have by the year 2000 A.D. Here we find a country in which the people have developed a great faith in material progress. Because technology has advanced so rapidly in the past fifty years, leaders in the various walks of life are devoting a great deal of time and money planning for the years immediately ahead. Specific industries are spending millions of dollars investigating the possibilities of the future, as are branches of the Armed Forces, several nonprofit foundations, various universities, and professional associations. By 2000 A.D. the United States will probably have a population of 330 million. These people will have to be housed, transported, fed, entertained, cared for medically, and educated in large supercities and their environs. The threat of greater stress and strain looms large, unless greater "creature comforts" can be provided, and unless life can be made meaningful. It seems imperative to devise better uses of leisure, because there seems to be every likelihood that a great many men and women will have to be paid to be idle—idle, that is, from today's standpoint. And yet those who are brighter and more energetic, and who desire responsibility, recognition, and power, will seemingly gain such rewards only through work. Where does education fit into the picture?

At present there are approximately 55 million young people enrolled at some level of our vast educational system, and the fantastic sum of 42 billion dollars a year is being spent to finance this gigantic enterprise. Unfortunately, however, many people are not happy with this situation. The enormity of the structure is staggering and almost imcomprehensible to any one individual or group. Of course, debate about what should comprise a fine education is entirely healthy. Naturally enough, many of the same questions have been asked and debated since so-called educational progress began: How can we determine what is a good education (*i.e.*, what criteria shall we employ?)? How should the current situation modify educational practice? What type of environment should be provided to guarantee the best educational outcome? And, specifically, what is the function of the school?

Throughout the course of history until the Golden Age of Greece, a good education had been a traditional education based on the transmission of the cultural heritage and the society's particular methods of survival. The Greeks, however, became so prosperous that for the first time it was possible, for a few at least, to depart from previous educational norms. Plato proposed an educational scheme in *The Republic* in which the Greeks might look forward to an ideal society. But the populace was not ready to put this proposal into practice, nor to accept Socrates' critical approach to current educational practice. Even the great Aristotle took sides against Plato in this respect. In his *Politics* he called for an educational pattern conforming to the actual political state in existence.

Throughout the Roman Empire and the Middle Ages such practices continued, despite the fact that from time to time certain educational theorists offered proposals of greater or lesser radical quality. Thus, when a society declined, those involved in the educational system had no ideas about societal rejuvenation and were in no position to be of significant assistance. During the Renaissance new ideas and practices developed outside of the traditional educational pattern. Then, later, after Humanism had made itself a strong force and had brought about the inauguration of a special school to foster its spirit, the introduction of science into the curriculum faced the same barriers all over again.

As Brubacher points out, this pattern continued in the eighteenth through the twentieth centuries as political and economic revolutions took place (1966, pp. 584–87). The school always played "the secondary rather than the primary role ... in periods of social transition." This was true in the French Revolution, the American Revolution, the Industrial Revolution in England, the Russian Revolution, and the several upheavals in Germany and Italy—even, to a great degree, in the so-called period of progressive education in the United States in the twentieth century! All of which leads to the conclusion that political leaders have never in world history viewed the school as an agent of social reconstruction.

Yet in modern history there have been a number of educators who believed strongly that the school was not living up to its potential in the preparation of the young for future leadership roles. Such people as the Marquis de Condorcet, Adrien Helvétius, Immanuel Kant, Jean Jacques Rousseau, Johann Heinrich Pestalozzi, Wilhelm August Froebel, Horace Mann, John Dewey, and George S. Counts have seen the need for the schools to serve a more creative function—to provide young people with the knowledge, understanding, and attitudes whereby they could more effectively lead the way in the ameliorotion of society. Such an approach would require great understanding on the part of an enlightened citizenry and complete academic freedom. The most controversial of issues would be the order of the day in such a school environment, and infinitely greater respect and confidence would have to be accorded to the teaching profession. This is not to say, of course, that great progress has not been made in regard to the matter of academic freedom; however, such freedom has been gained for the most part at great personal loss to individual teachers.

The question whether our educational institutions have made progress insofar as quantity and quality are concerned must be considered briefly. The almost self-evident answer is yes, even in those countries that have not provided educational opportunities for more than a selected minority. In the United States more than forty-five per cent are presently going on to some form of higher education. Of course, there are some who contend that it is wrong to have approximately five "levels" of higher education ranging from community colleges to select Ivy League institutions. When this question is raised, the emphasis in the discussion necessarily shifts from quantity to quality—to a degree at least. With societies changing their economies, and often their political regimes, from one type to another, the body of knowledge has grown and the curriculum has expanded immeasurably. Knowledge about the teaching and learning process has also expanded, but not to the same measure. The cost of new facilities and equipment now comprises more than half of the community's operational budget—the largest item!

Even with all this advancement there are many who are not satisfied with the quality of education being offered our young people. Their main reason is that the school's end product is not the most "desirable"; enter the question of educational philosophy! Determining a hierarchy of educational values is most difficult in a pluralistic society such as ours. As encouraged as we might be by the fact that the individual and his personality counts for more in the United States today than perhaps ever before in the history of man, we are still confronted by the ever-present struggle between educational essentialists and educational progressivists. The one thing that we can be really thankful for is that our type of society allows us the freedom for such continuing debate.

THE NEED FOR CONSENSUS

From the standpoint of educational philosophy, therefore, any evaluation of qualitative as opposed to quantitative progress would depend upon the extent to which educational practice approximated a particular philosophical ideal. Therefore, your personal decision about progress that our field may have made in solving the specific persistent problems enumerated in this volume can't help but be highly subjective. *Your personal evaluation should be based on the philosophical tendency to which you subscribe.* Naturally it will be conditioned by your personal background and experiences—including the scientific evidence available—that have caused you to develop a set of attitudes. Professional maturity depends upon a sound philosophical base.

Philosophical investigation of a normative and analytical nature over the past eight years within this and related fields has convinced the writer of the vital importance of a continuing search for, *and* the possibility of, consensus among the conflicting philosophies of physical, health, and recreation education in the Western world. We have been proceeding "amoeba-like" for so long with our own biased and eclectic statements of philosophical position that even the current attempt to delineate *our own* individual positions represents a vast improvement. These words are not meant to be derogatory of any one individual, or groups of individuals; such philosophical ineptitude is actually characteristic of the large majority of practitioners in the educational world.

The difficulty of achieving consensus is exactly the problem. It is really questionable, although this writer is sufficiently reconstructionistic in his personal philosophy to believe in such approaches strongly, whether the American Association for Health, Physical Education, and Recreation can hope to achieve true consensus by the typical conferences that are held periodically. With such a careful effort being made to have both sexes, all educational levels, the various educational agencies, and other related groups represented, such meetings usually result in a group in which progressive Christian idealists and pragmatic experimentalists (including a few reconstructionists) predominate, and only a sprinkling of naturalistic realists, rational humanists, and moderate (Catholic) realists is evident. The outcome of any such deliberations is consequently predetermined. If a vote on an issue is taken, the realists are hopelessly outnumbered. When the conference report is published, "complete loyalty to God, mother, and country" is proclaimed resoundingly, the progressivist banner is gallantly waved, and there is just enough of an "eclectic taint" to the entire document that the realist, who might well have conceived of such a conference as "pooled ignorance" anyhow, acts blithely disinterested or is perhaps sullen but not actively mutinous about the end result.

It is fortunate that there is *more agreement in practice than in theory*. From another standpoint, also, a certain amount of agreement in theory at least is necessary in order to disagree. To make *any* progress there must be agreement on the issues and on an interpretation of the rules for debate. Lastly, it can be said that it would be a rather dull world if there were complete agreement on all issues at all times.

There are actually a number of methods available by which greater consensus can be achieved. A formidable task, but perhaps not an impossible one, is to attempt to break down communications barriers. The study of semantics, the language analysis movement in philosophy, and the developing social science of administration should tremendously expedite the matter. The development of a truly international language, taught in all countries in conjunction with the mother tongue, would be an enormous aid to communication as well.

It is interesting and important to note that there are some common presuppositions among the different educational philosophies; in fact, among these rival philosophies there are definite points of agreement, as well as large areas in which many points are somewhat similar and often overlapping. In the field of education, for example, some of the areas of practical agreement are that 1) the safety of the child is basic; 2) the school has a responsibility to provide a health service unit; 3) teachers need a certain educational background and experience; 4) boys and girls should be educated for at least a certain period of time; and 5) there are certain "cardinal principles" of education. *The Central Purpose of American Education,* published by the Educational Policies Commission, after reaffirming earlier statements of 1918 and 1938, states a central purpose—the development of the ability to think, which is not meant to be thought of as exclusive (1961, p. 12).

The extent of class involvement in the discussion of controversial issues is one area where there is a difference of opinion. Many would argue that the student should be free to arrive at a solution, but it is recognized that he'll have to be careful in many situations about how he expresses himself in certain areas of politics, religion, or problems of a particular social nature. It could be stated further that race heritage ought to be the common heritage of all, but the difficulty comes when we get down to the specifics of how much race experience should be included in the curriculum, or what should be emphasized, or how it should be taught. And so it goes as increasingly less consensus is apparent (Brubacher, 1962, pp. 350–54).

What common denominators may be found in the specialized field of physical education and sport, in health and safety education, or in recreation education? The answer to this question might be as follows:

1. The belief of the large majority of physical educators that *regular* physical education periods should be *required* for all school children through grades ten or eleven.

2. The importance of a child developing certain attitudes toward his own health in particular and toward community health in general.

3. Leisure should be put to worthy use. It is understood that in America many people are presumably enjoying a greater amount of leisure than has ever been available before.

4. Physical vigor is extremely important, but there is no general agreement among the men, or between men and women in the profession, about what really constitutes physical fitness. There are national norms, but no national standards (or agreement on whether there should be standards).

5. There should be an experience in competitive athletics. This applies both to boys and girls, but the amount of emphasis and the time when this should be made available are points of contention.

6. Boys and girls who need therapeutic exercise for remediable physical defects should be helped.

7. Character and personality development is important. We believe generally that our specialized field can make a definite contribution toward the achievement of this objective, but we have very little scientific evidence to support this claim.

Having stated these common denominators, it would appear that the time for a consensus *on what it is that we do* is long overdue.[1]

The potentialities for pure and applied research in physical, health, and recreation education (including sport and competitive athletics) are limitless.

---

[1] *The Contribution of Physical Activity to Human Well-Being* was seemingly as important a project as AAHPER's Research Council, or the Association itself, has ever undertaken (*Research Quarterly*, **XXXI**, 2, Part II, May 1960). This type of endeavor must be updated, "sharpened," and clarified regularly with a format similar to that of the recent publication, *Human Behavior: An Inventory of Scientific Findings* by Berelson and Steiner (1964).

The unique nature of the field and its role in man's education relates quite obviously to physiology, anatomy, psychology, sociology, history, philosophy, anthropology, chemistry, medicine, economics, political science, and administrative theory. If we are completely honest we will have to admit that there are only relatively few *qualified* researchers possessing "physical educator's hearts" (*i.e.*, people with professional preparation in physical, health, and recreation education, with *sound* backgrounds in at least one of the fields mentioned above, with a knowledge of research method and appropriate techniques, and who are really interested in this field and its future). Many more bright, idealistic young people seek admittance to the field, but the quality of our undergraduate and graduate programs of professional preparation, *including our research efforts,* must be improved immeasurably. Time is running short!

Epilogue

It is a rare week that goes by when I do not talk to some young man (or woman) about his future in physical education—whether he wants to be a teacher and coach, or to become actively involved in some other facet within the field. When he asks what the future holds in store for him as a physical educator, I suppose I should reply that he holds his own future *and* that of the field in his hands. Life is what *we* make it.

But such a reply smacks of an idealism that we, in more pessimistic moments, view as passé. Today the average physical education student is typically realistic and often quite materialistic as well. The young man contemplating a major in physical education probably makes this decision on the basis of his athletic experience with a high school coach. He has admired his coach very much. He has assessed his own personal athletic ability, his liking of people, and perhaps his scholastic attainment—or lack of it because of poor study habits. Then, often against the presumably better judgment of his parents, he makes up his mind to be a coach and a physical educator in that order. He sees himself coaching a successful high school football or basketball team, and then possibly going on to bigger and better things as a college coach.

As a counselor, my task is to explain to this young man in a few well-chosen words that the field of physical, health, and recreation education is much more than simply being an athletic coach, as important a task as that can be. This is very difficult, and I am not always certain just how much to say. I don't want to bore him with my experiences in the various aspects of the field, including coaching. So much depends on his prior experiences. I usually tell him about the advantages and the disadvantages emphasizing the former more than the latter. I conclude by telling him that, even though he may have heard that the field is overcrowded for men at the present, there is ample room for a well-qualified, conscientious, devoted professional educator. As he is leaving, I tell him to keep in touch and not to hesitate to contact me or my close associate if he has a problem, and I wish him good luck.

But after he leaves, I begin to wonder if I have said and done the right things. Of course, perhaps nothing I could have said or done would change his thinking radically. I do hope sincerely that his university experience will be such that he will emerge upon graduation as a fine, competent young teacher of physical education ready to assume professional leadership of the highest type.

What happens to this young man? Many influences affect his development, both good and bad. Eventually he acquires certain knowledge, competencies, and skills. He may be a good student, a fair student, or a poor student. Rarely is he an outstanding student. He develops a set of attitudes. Only very occasionally does he show an inclination after graduation to be really active in at least one professional organization in his chosen field. I wonder where he has failed—where *we* have failed.

The large majority of physical educators haven't had the opportunity, or haven't taken the time, to work out their own personal philosophies. Granted that along the way there has been a great deal of discussion about aims and objectives, but it has usually been carried out in such a helter-skelter fashion that they want no more of it. They are anxious to learn the much more tangible competencies and skills that they can use on the job. And so they leave us as graduates not really knowing why they are doing anything and where they are going, so to speak.

Physical educators need exactly the same sort of progression in history, philosophy, and administration of physical education and sport that they usually follow in anatomy and physiology and the subsequent applied aspects of these subjects. Any person striving to function intelligently in society needs an understanding of the historical foundations of our society and of education in our society. He will then be able to study and fully appreciate the historical backgrounds of his own field and the persistent problems that have been faced through the ages. Secondly, a professional person needs a philosophy of life and/or religion. Do our professional students ever take an introductory course in philosophy or in the philosophy of religion? Except for those majoring in physical education in Catholic universities, perhaps not one in a thousand has had this opportunity!

Furthermore, a teacher of physical, health, and recreation education should have a philosophy of education in harmony with his philosophy of life. Strangely enough, however, philosophy of education courses are often available only as an elective and our students "studiously" try to avoid them. The culmination of this recommended curricular sequence (prior to a course in administration) should be an outstanding course in the philosophy of physical, health, and recreation education—a course in which the prospective teacher begins to develop a personal philosophy relating to his specialized field that does not clash with his basic beliefs about life and education. The achievement of a "stage of philosophical maturity" may well become a life-long task. The reflective thought required to accomplish this task is a mighty cheap price to pay for a well-ordered life.

We have only to look at our present programs with their shifting emphases to realize that we are, to a large degree, vacillating practitioners. This is true both within the school and in public recreation. If we ever hope to convince ourselves, our colleagues in education, and the informed portion of the general public of our worth, we should as individual professionals at least determine whether we are truly progressivistic or truly essentialistic in our philosophical tendencies, and then work from there. We simply can't continue as dilettantes or casual eclectics ready to jump in any direction when the prevailing wind blows.

No matter which stage of philosophical development you may have achieved presently—the "ostrich stage," the "cafeteria stage," the "fence-sitter stage," the stage of early maturity, or the stage of philosophical maturity—you may find it necessary to retrace your steps before you can truly build your own personal philosophy logically, consistently, and systematically. Obviously, there is no hard and fast progression to which you *must* adhere. Through the use of the self-evaluation checklist which follows, you may discover that you are quite "pure" already. At any rate, find out where you stand and take up the philosophic quest from there. You simply can't go wrong, *if* you go about it honestly, sincerely, and diligently. People of all ages are searching for meaningful values in their lives. If you help them in just one area, that of physical, health, and recreation education, you will have attained the highest of professional goals.

appendix a

PHILOSOPHY OF PHYSICAL, HEALTH, AND RECREATION EDUCATION:
A Professional Checklist *

I. *The Nature of Reality (Metaphysics)*

a. _____ Nature is an emergent evolution, and man's frame of reality is limited to nature as it functions. The world is characterized by activity and change. Rational man has developed through organic evolution, and the world is yet incomplete—a reality that is constantly undergoing change because of a theory of emergent novelty. Man enjoys freedom of will; freedom is achieved through continuous and developmental learning from experience.

b. _____ Mind as experienced by all men is basic and real. The entire universe is mind essentially. Man is more than just a body; he possesses a soul, and such possession makes him of a higher order than all other creatures on earth. "The order of the world is due to the manifestation in space and time of an eternal and spiritual reality." The individual is part of the whole, and it is man's task to learn as much about the Absolute as possible. There is divided opinion within this position regarding the problem of monism or pluralism. Man has freedom to determine which way he shall go in life; he can relate to the moral law in the universe, or he can turn against it.

c. _____ Experience and nature "constitute both the form and content of the entire universe" (multiverse?). There is no such thing as a pre-established order of things in the world. Reality is evolving, and humanity appears to be a most important manifestation of the natural process. The impact of cultural forces upon man are fundamental, and every effort must be made to understand them as we strive to build the best type of a group-centered culture. In other words, "the structure of cultural reality" should be our foremost concern. Cultural determinants have shaped the history of man, and he has now reached a crucial stage in the development of life on this planet. Our efforts should be focused on the building of a world culture.

d. _____ "The world exists in itself, apart from our desires and knowledges." There is only one reality; that which we perceive. "The universe is made up of real substantial entities, existing in themselves and ordered to one another by extramental relations. . . ." Some feel that there is a basic unity present, while others believe in a nonunified cosmos with two or more substances or processes at work. Things don't just happen; they happen because many interrelated forces make them occur in a particular way. Man lives within this world of cause and effect, and he simply cannot make things happen independent of it.

---

* *Instructions:* Read the statements carefully and indicate by an (X) that statement in each question which seems *closest* to your own personal belief. Check answers only after all six questions have been completed.

II. *Educational Aims and Objectives*

a. _____ "A philosophy holding that the aim of education is the acquisition of verified knowledge of the environment; recognizes the value of content as well as the activities involved in learning, and takes into account the external determinants of human behavior . . . Education is the acquisition of the art of the utilization of knowledge." The primary task of education is to transmit knowledge, without which civilization cannot continue to flourish. Whatever man has discovered to be true because it conforms to reality must be handed down to future generations as the social or cultural tradition. Some holding this philosophy believe that the good life emanates from cooperation with God's grace and that development of the Christian virtues is obviously of greater worth than learning or anything else.

b. _____ Social self-realization is the supreme value in education. The realization of this ideal is most important for the individual in his social setting— a world culture. Positive ideals should be molded toward the evolving democratic ideal by a general education which is group-centered and in which the majority determines the acceptable goals. Education by means of "hidden coercion" is to be scrupulously avoided. Learning is explained by the organismic principle of functional psychology. Social intelligence acquired teaches man to control and direct his urges as he concurs with or attempts to modify cultural purposes.

c. _____ Through education the developing organism becomes what it latently is. All education may be said to have a religious significance, which means that there is a "moral imperative" on education. As man's mind strives to realize itself, there is the possibility of realization of the Absolute within the individual mind. Education should aid the child to adjust to the basic realities (the spiritual ideals of truth, beauty, and goodness) that the history of the race has furnished us. The basic values of human living are health, character, social justice, skill, art, love, knowledge, philosophy, and religion.

d. _____ The general aim of education is more education. "Education in the broadest sense can be nothing else than the changes made in human beings by their experience." Participation by students in the formation of aims and objectives is absolutely essential to generate the all-important desired interest. Social efficiency can well be considered the general aim of education. Pupil growth is a paramount goal, as the individual is placed at the center of the educational experience.

III. *The Educative Process (Epistemology)*

a. _____ An organismic approach to the learning process is basic. Thought cannot be independent of certain aspects of the organism; it is related integrally to emotional and muscular functions. Man's mind enables him to cope with the problems of human life in a social environment. Social intelligence is closely related to scientific method. Certain operational concepts, inseparable from metaphysics and axiology (beliefs about reality and values), focus on the reflective thought, problem solving, and social consensus necessary for the transformation of the culture.

b. _____ Knowledge is the result of a process of thought with a useful purpose. Truth is not only to be tested by its correspondence with reality, but also by its practical results. Knowledge is earned through experience and is an instrument of verification. Mind has evolved in the natural order as a more flexible means whereby man adapts himself to his world. Learning takes place when interest and effort unite to produce the desired result. A psychological order (problem solving as explained through scientific method) is more useful than a logical arrangement (from the simple fact to the complex conclusion). There is always a social context to learning, and the curriculum must be adapted to the particular society for which it is intended.

c. _____ Understanding the nature of knowledge will clarify the nature of reality. Nature is the medium by which the Absolute communicates to us. Basically, knowledge comes only from the mind—a mind which must offer and receive ideas. Mind and matter are qualitatively different. A finite mind emanates through heredity from another finite mind. Thought is the standard by which all else in the world is judged. An individual attains truth for himself by examining the wisdom of the past through his own mind. Reality, viewed in this way, is a system of logic and order that has been established by the Universal Mind. Experimental testing helps to determine what the truth really is.

d. _____ There are two major epistemological theories of knowledge in this position. One states that the aim of knowledge "is to bring into awareness the object as it really is." The other emphasizes that objects are "represented" in man's consciousness, not "presented." Students should develop habits and skills involved with acquiring knowledge, with using knowledge practically to meet life's problems, and with realizing the enjoyment that life offers. A second variation of epistemological belief indicates that the child develops his intellect by employing reason to learn a subject. The principal educational aims here must be the same for all men at all times in all places. Others carry this further and state that education is the process by which man seeks to link himself ultimately with his Creator.

IV. *Values in Specialized Field* (*Physical Education*)

a. _____ I believe in the concept of "total fitness" implied in an educational design pointed toward the individual's self-realization as a social being. In our field there should be opportunity for selection of a wide variety of useful activities. Instruction in motor skills is necessary to provide a sufficient amount of "physical" fitness activity. The introduction of dance and art into physical education can contribute to man's creative expression. Intramural sports and voluntary recreational activities should be stressed. This applies especially to team competition, with particular stress on cooperation and promotion of friendly competition. Extramural sport competition can be introduced when there is a need; striving for excellence is important, but it is more important to keep materialistic influence out of educational programs. Relaxation techniques should have a place, as should the whole concept of education for leisure.

b. _____ I am extremely interested in individual personality development. I believe in education "of the physical," and yet I believe in education "through the physical" as well. Nevertheless, I do see physical education as important but occupying a "lower rung on the educational ladder." I believe that desirable objectives for physical education would include the development of responsible citizenship and group participation. In competitive sport, I believe that the transfer of training theory is in operation in connection with the development of desirable personality traits, but sports participation should always be a means not an end.

c. _____ I am much more interested in promoting the concept of total fitness rather than physical fitness alone. I believe that physical education should be an integral subject in the curriculum. Students should have the opportunity to select a wide variety of useful activities, many of which should help to develop "social intelligence." The activities offered should bring natural impulses into play. To me, physical education classes and intramural sports are more important to the large majority of students than interscholastic or intercollegiate sports and deserve priority if conflict arises over budgetary allotment, staff availability, or use of facilities. I can, however, give full support to team experiences in competitive sports, because they can be vital educational experiences if properly conducted.

d. _____ I believe that education "of the physical" should have primary emphasis in our field. I am concerned with the development of physical vigor, and such development should have priority over the recreational aspects of physical education. Many people, who believe in the same educational philosophy as I do, recommend that all students in public schools should have a daily period designed to strengthen their muscles and develop their bodily coordination. Physical education, of course, must yield precedence to intellectual education. I give "qualified approval" to interscholastic athletics since they do help with the learning of sportsmanship and desirable social conduct if properly conducted. But all these things, with the possible exception of physical training, are definitely extracurricular.

V. *Values in Specialized Field (School Health Education)*

a. _____ I believe that man should be a "rugged animal," and this standard should apply to girls as well as boys. Health, as I see it, is a primary objective of education, and the child needs health instruction. The success of the school health education program depends upon the degree of cooperation among home, school, and community agencies. An educated person must understand the difference between health and disease, and he must know how to protect and improve his own health, that of his dependents, and that of the community. As I see it, the program of school health, physical education, and recreation may be administered as a unified program within a school system. I believe that natural types of exercise promote sound mental health. All these aspects of the total program may be coordinated because they are related in many ways. Through unity, these subdivisions could probably serve the needs of school children and youth much more effectively than is often the case at the present. To be truly effective, school health education must be concerned with helping the individual to lead a rich, full life. This means more than providing a health service so that students can maintain minimum health needed to "pursue intellectual work with the least amount of strain." Health should be defined positively—as that quality which enables us "to live most and serve best."

b. _____ I believe in the development of physical vigor and health. There is no question in my mind but that the school should provide "an atmosphere conducive to both emotional and physical health." Furthermore, "knowledge about the principles of physical and emotional health is a proper ingredient of the curriculum." I believe that the community does have a responsibility to provide "clinical facilities for therapy," "but this does not mean that they are part of the school program or curriculum any more than are the boilers in heating systems." I assert that the home must have the complete responsibility for assisting youth to acquire desirable health habits —that is, unless we wish to establish some form of community youth organizations to accomplish this end. "The health of adolescents is for the most part too good and their sources of energy are too great to make health problems real to them." In similar vein, sex education is certainly not a proper function of the school. It is not logical that teaching the means for securing health values would be complete anyhow until the perspective from which they are viewed is also taught; this perspective is found only in the humanities—in literature, art, religion, and philosophy. In summary, therefore, every person needs a basic core of knowledge in order to lead a human life, and this includes the learning of health knowledge. This is consistent with the central purpose of the school—the development of the individual's rational powers.

c. _____ I believe that health is a basic value of human living and that the truly educated individual should be "physically fit," should live "near the maximum of his efficiency," and should have "a body which is the ready servant of his will." But even though I believe health is a value basic to all the others, I would have to place it at the bottom of the hierarchy of educational values. Worship must be placed at the top, because through it man is brought "into conscious relation to the infinite spirit of the universe. . . ." Thus, health would not be included in a listing of the "essential studies" of the curriculum except where it would probably be included incidentally under biology. However, I am interested in "building wholeness of mind and body," "the development of strong, healthy bodies, good habits of mental and physical health," "and the right start in the teaching of health, safety, and physical education to children." There is no question in my mind but that educators should work for a larger measure of integration in the individual by promoting "more intensive study of the body, leading to scientific knowledge: anatomy, body chemistry, hygiene, physiology, etc.; and attention to sex characteristics and habits, leading to a greater understanding of the place of sex in human life, with implications for hygiene. . . ." But such knowledge is made available to boys and girls, and young men and women, as a "service" program in the schools—a service is provided to man, and through this contribution to his health he is enabled to pursue higher educational goals.

d. _____ As I see it, there can be no such thing as a fixed or universal curriculum in physical, health, and recreation education. Men and women should be sturdy and possess vigorous health. Positive health should be a primary educational aim. Such a program would necessitate the cooperative involvement of many agencies. Health knowledge and attitudes should be realized through the provision of experiences involving problem solving. "Direct" health instruction should be offered, but such learning can take place indirectly in the science curriculum. Sex education and family relations instruction are very important. Instruction in mental hygiene needs serious attention in our highly complex society.

VI. *Values in Recreation (Education)*

a. _____ I believe that the role of play and recreation in the development of personality and the "perfectly integrated individual" is looming larger with each passing year and that it has not been fully understood or appreciated in the past. For this reason it seems quite logical to me that education should reassess the contributions that recreation and play do make in the education of man. That there is a need for educational research along these lines is self-evident. I believe further that we should examine very closely any theories of play and recreation which grant educational possibilities to these activities of man. The self-expression theory of play suggests that man's chief need in life is to achieve the satisfaction and accomplishment of self-expression of one's own personality. Here is an explanation that seems to consider quite fully the conception of man as an organic unity—a total organism. I believe that man is a purposive being who is striving to achieve those values which are embedded in reality itself. To the extent that we can realize the eternal values through the choice of the right kinds of play and recreation without flouting the moral order in the world, we should be progressive enough to disregard a dualistic theory of work and play. Another difficulty that confronts us is differentiating between physical education and recreation. Recreation has developed to the point where it is now clearly one of our major social institutions. I believe that recreation can make a contribution to the development of an "integrated individual in an integrated society growing in the image of the integrated universe." Mankind today is actually faced with a "recreational imperative."

b. _____ I believe it is difficult to separate the objectives of recreation education from physical education when physical activities are being considered. Within the schools I recommend a unified approach for physical, health, and recreation education. In this discussion I am only including those recreational activities which are "physical" in nature. All these leisure activities should be available to all on a year-round basis. I see recreation education as a legitimate phase of the core curriculum but would include further recreational opportunities as well as opportunity for relaxation later in the day.

c. _____ As I see it, work and play are sharply differentiated in life. Play serves a most useful purpose at recess or after school, but it should *not* be part of the regular curriculum. I believe that the use of leisure is significant to the development of our culture, but I realize today that winning the Cold War is going to take a lot more hard work and somewhat less leisure. I see leisure pursuits or experience as an opportunity to get relief from work while also being re-creative. The surplus energy theory of play and recreation makes sense to me. So does the more recent bio-social theory of play—the idea that play helps the organism to achieve balance. I feel that the "play attitude" is missing almost completely in many organized sports. Play (and recreation) is, therefore, very important to me; I believe it should be "liberating" to the individual. People can develop their potentialities for wholesome hobbies through recreation. Furthermore, recreation can serve as a "safety valve" by the reduction of the psychic tensions which are evidently caused by so many of life's typical stresses. Even though play should *not* be considered as a basic part of the curriculum, we should not forget that it provides an "indispensable seasoning" to the good life. Extracurricular play and recreational activities and a sound general education should suffice to equip the student for leisure activities in our society.

d. _____ I am inclined to favor the adoption of the name recreation education for the field. I see advantages in a unified approach whereby the three specialized areas of health, physical education, and recreation (in schools) would provide a variety of experiences that will enable the individual to live a richer, fuller life through superior adjustment to his environment. I believe that education for the worthy use of leisure is basic to the curriculum of the school—a curriculum in which pupil growth, broadly defined, is all-important. Secondly, play shall be conducted in such a way that desirable moral growth will be fostered. Thirdly, overorganized sport competition is not true recreation, since the welfare of the individual is often submerged in the extreme emphasis frequently placed on winning. I believe it is a mistake to confuse the psychological distinction between work and play with the traditional economic distinction. All citizens should have ample opportunity to use their free time in a creative and fruitful manner. I do not condemn a person who watches others perform with a high level of skill in any of our cultural recreational activities, including sport, so long as the individual keeps such viewing in a balanced role in his entire life.

Answers: (Read only after all six questions are completed.)

I. The Nature of Reality (Metaphysics)

   a. Experimentalism (Pragmatic Naturalism)
   b. Idealism
   c. Reconstructionism
   d. Realism

II. Educational Aims and Objectives

   a. Realism
   b. Reconstructionism
   c. Idealism
   d. Experimentalism

III. The Educative Process (Epistemology)

   a. Reconstructionism
   b. Experimentalism
   c. Idealism
   d. Realism

IV. Physical Education

   a. Reconstructionism
   b. Idealism
   c. Experimentalism
   d. Realism

V. School Health Education

   a. Experimentalism
   b. Realism
   c. Idealism
   d. Reconstructionism

VI. Recreation (Education)

   a. Idealism
   b. Reconstructionism
   c. Realism
   d. Experimentalism

THE EDUCATIONAL
PHILOSOPHY OF
EXISTENTIALISM
With Implications for Physical,
Health, and Recreation Education

The Nature of Reality (Metaphysics)

The world of material objects extended in mathematical space with only quantitative and measurable properties is not the world we live in as human beings; our world is a human world, not a world of science. From this human context all the abstractions of science ultimately derive their meaning. Man is first and foremost a concrete involvement within the world, and we distinguish the opposed poles of body and mind. Existence precedes essence; man decides his own fate. His self-transcendence distinguishes him from all other animals, and he cannot be understood in his totality by the natural sciences. Truth is expressed in art and religion, as well as in science. Time and history are fundamental dimensions of human existence. The basic human task is for man to become an authentic individual in his own right. Life's present conditions can be transformed by man, an animal who stands open to the future. (Paraphrased from William Barrett.)

Educational Aims and Objectives

The existentialist is cognizant of the fact that the socialization of the child has become an equally important educational goal as his intellectual development. He is concerned, however, because the leading educational theories "see" the young as "things to be worked over in some fashion to bring them into alignment with a prior notion of what they *should* be." Even the experimentalists seem to have failed in their effort to bring "the learner into a self-determining posture." Assuming there is general agreement that a set of fundamental dispositions is to be formed, should the criterion used for the evaluation of the worth of individual dispositions be "public rather than a personal and private criterion?" "If education is to be truly human, it must somehow *awaken awareness* in the learner—existential awareness of himself as a single subjectivity in the world." Students should "constantly, freely, baselessly, and creatively" choose their individual pattern of education. The subjectivity of the existentialistic learner should thrive in the arts (music, painting, poetry, and creative writing, etc.), but similar possibilities to study human motivation are available in the social sciences as well. (Paraphrased from Van Cleve Morris.)

The Educative Process (Epistemology)

Childhood is viewed as a "pre-existential phase of human life." About the time of puberty in the individual, there is an "existential moment" in the young person's subjective life. It is the time of the "onset of the self's awareness of its own existing." For the first time, the "individual sees himself as responsible for his own conduct." Then, and only then, "education must become an act of discovery." The learner's experience must be such that he gets "personally implicated in the subject matter and in the situation around him." Knowledge must be "chosen, *i.e.*, appropriated, before it can be true for that consciousness." It isn't something that is purely objective, nor is it merely purposeful. Knowledge "becomes knowledge only when a subjectivity takes hold of it and puts it into his own life." It could be argued that "the existentialist has little to offer in the way of a method of knowing." Whether we are considering logic, scientific evidence, sense perception, intuition, or revelation, "it is the individual self which must make the ultimate decision as to what is, as a matter of fact, true." Perceptually and cognitively, the individual is aware of the objects of existence, but there is something more—an "internal, subjective awareness"—which enables him to know that he knows. Psychology seems to have given very few answers about this latter phase of the epistemological process to date. (Paraphrased from Van Cleve Morris.)

Physical, Health, and Recreation Education (Aims and Objectives)

This field should strive to fulfill a role in the general educational pattern of arts and sciences. The goal is *total fitness*—not just physical fitness—with a balance between activities emphasizing competition and cooperation. The concept of "universal man" is paramount, but we must allow the individual the opportunity to choose for himself based on self-evaluation, knowledge, skills, and attitudes. We should help the child who is "authentically eccentric" feel at home in the physical education activities program. We should further devise opportunities for youth to commit themselves to values and people. An important question in sport and athletics is how may we preserve the individual's authenticity in individual, dual, and team sports where winning is so often overemphasized. In sport, as opposed to competitive athletics, a person may personally select the values he derives from activity. We should play, therefore, for actualization of self—an attempt to use sport for our own purposes. Physical activities such as modern dance, in which the opportunity for creativity is so important, should be stressed. (E.F.Z.)

The educational process itself should be natural—a give-and-take situation. The student should be allowed to observe and to inquire freely. Freedom is most important, but the teacher is needed as the student can't teach himself. A good teacher should show passion, but he should not be egocentric nor too biased about a system or a point of view. He should be completely dedicated to the search for truth and to the need to develop a "self-moving" individual. Typically, the search for truth is an individual matter, but majority opinion should be tested when action is needed in a group situation. The student should develop an "orderly mind"; he should be willing to debate issues; and he should strive to be creative. Education has not been successful if the student becomes a carbon copy of his teacher. This methodology should characterize the physical educator's teaching and coaching. (Paraphrased from Ralph Harper.)

In regard to health and recreation education, much of what has been stated above should apply. The child must develop an awareness of the need for self-education about the various aspects of personal and community health. Controversial issues should never be avoided. All types of recreational needs and interests should be met through recreation education. One function of play is personal liberation and release. All sorts of group recreational activities are fine, and have a place, but opportunities for *individual* expression should not be downgraded. (E.F.Z.)

General
Bibliography

Ainsworth, Dorothy S., "The History of Physical Education in Colleges for Women." Ph.D. dissertation, Columbia University, 1930.

Alston, William P., *Philosophy of Language*. Englewood Cliffs, N.J.: Prentice-Hall, Inc., 1964.

American Association for Health, Physical Education, and Recreation, Division for Girls' and Women's Sports, "State of Policies and Procedures for Competition in Girls' and Women's Sports," *JOHPER*, 28, No. 6 (September, 1957), 57–58.

American Association for Health, Physical Education, and Recreation, Division for Girls' and Women's Sports and Division of Men's Athletics, *Values in Sports*. Washington, D.C.: *AAHPER*, 1963.

Aron, Raymond, *Introduction to Philosophy of History* (Rev. ed.). Boston: The Beacon Press, 1948. (English translation, 1961).

Ashton, Dudley, "Contributions of Dance to Physical Education, Part I," *JOHPER*, 26, No. 9 (December, 1955).

———, "Contributions of Dance to Physical Education, Part II," *JOHPER*, 27, No. 4 (April, 1956).

Avery, Catherine B., ed. *Classical Handbook*. New York: Appleton-Century-Crofts, Inc., 1962.

Bair, Donn E., "An Identification of Some Philosophical Beliefs Held by Influential Professional Leaders in American Physical Education." Ph.D. dissertation, University of Southern California, 1956.

Ballou, Ralph B., "An Analysis of the Writings of Selected Church Fathers to A.D. 394 to Reveal Attitudes Regarding Physical Activity." Ph.D. dissertation, University of Oregon, 1965.

Barrett, William, *Irrational Man: A Study in Existential Philosophy*. New York: Doubleday & Company, Inc., 1958.

Barrows, I. C., *Physical Training*. Boston: Press of George H. Ellis, 1899.

Bayles, Ernest E., *Pragmatism in Education*. New York: Harper & Row, Publishers, 1966.

Beck, Robert N., *Perspectives in Philosophy*. New York: Holt, Rinehart and Winston, Inc., 1961.

Bennett, Bruce L., "The Life of Dudley Allen Sargent, M.D., and His Contributions to Physical Education." Ph.D. dissertation, The University of Michigan, 1947.

Bennett, Bruce L., "Religion and Physical Education." A paper presented at the Cincinnati Convention of the AAHPER, April 10, 1962.

Bennett, Patricia, "The History and Objectives of the National Section for Girls' and Women's Sports." Ed.D. dissertation, Mills College, 1956.

Boodin, John E., "Philosophy of History" in *Twentieth Century Philosophy,* ed. by D. D. Runes. New York: Philosophical Library, 1943.

Brameld, T., *Toward a Reconstructed Philosophy of Education.* New York: The Dryden Press, 1956.

Breed, Frederick S., "Education and the Realistic Outlook," in *Forty-First Yearbook* of the National Society for the Study of Education (Part I). Chicago, Ill.: The University of Chicago Press, 1942.

Breiner, Andrew H., "A Study of the Concerns of the College Physical Education Association over the Past Twenty-Five Years." Master's thesis, Ohio State University, 1956.

Brickman, W. W., *Guide to Research in Educational History.* New York: New York University Bookstore, 1949.

Brightbill, Charles K., *Man and Leisure: A Philosophy of Recreation.* Englewood Cliffs, N.J.: Prentice-Hall, Inc., 1961.

Bronson, Alice O., "Clark W. Hetherington: Scientist and Philosopher." Ph.D. dissertation, University of Utah, 1955.

Bronstein, D. J., and H. M. Schulweis, *Approaches to the Philosophy of Religion.* Englewood Cliffs, N.J.: Prentice-Hall, Inc., 1954.

Broudy, Harry S., *Building a Philosophy of Education* (2nd ed.). Englewood Cliffs, N.J.: Prentice-Hall, Inc., 1961.

Brubacher, John S., *A History of the Problems of Education* (2nd ed.). New York: McGraw-Hill Book Co., 1966.

————, *Modern Philosophies of Education* (3rd ed.). New York: McGraw-Hill Book Co., 1962.

Bucher, C. A., *Foundations of Physical Education* (3rd ed.). St. Louis: The C. V. Mosby Company, 1960.

Bury, J. B., *The Idea of Progress.* New York: Dover Publications, Inc., 1955.

Butler, J. Donald, *Four Philosophies* (Rev. ed.). New York: Harper & Row, Publishers, 1957.

————, *Idealism in Education.* New York: Harper & Row, Publishers, 1966.

Butts, R. F., *A Cultural History of Education.* New York: McGraw-Hill Book Co., 1947.

Cahn, L. Joseph, "Contributions of Plato to Thought on Physical Education." Ed.D. dissertation, New York University, 1941.

Carner, Julia, "A Study of the Influence of the Philosophy of the Church of Jesus Christ of Latter-day Saints on Physical Education in the Church Schools." Ph.D. dissertation, University of Oregon, 1964.

Carskadon, T. R., and G. Soule, *U.S.A. in New Dimensions.* New York: The Macmillan Company, 1957.

Cavanaugh, Patric L., "A Delineation of Moderate Realism and Physical Education." Ph.D. dissertation, The University of Michigan, 1967.

Champion, S. G., and D. Short, *Readings from World Religions.* Boston: The Beacon Press, 1951.

Clark, Margaret C. (now Oestreicher), "A Philosophical Interpretation of a Program of Physical Education in a State Teachers College." Ph.D. dissertation, New York University, 1943.

Clarke, H. Harrison, "Biographies of Fellows, American Academy of Physical Education." Eugene, Oregon: Health and Physical Education Microcards, 1953.

Cobb, Louise S., "A Study of the Functions of Physical Education in Higher Education." Ph.D. dissertation, Columbia University, 1943.

Commager, Henry Steele, "A Quarter Century—Its Advances," *Look,* 25, No. 10 (June 6, 1961), 80–91.

Cowell, Charles C., and Wellman L. France, *Philosophy and Principles of Physical Education.* Englewood Cliffs, N.J.: Prentice-Hall, Inc., 1963.

Cozens, F. W., and F. S. Stumpf, *Sports in American Life.* Chicago: The University of Chicago Press, 1953.

Cubberley, E. P., *Readings in the History of Education.* Boston: Houghton Mifflin Company, 1920.

———, *Readings in Public Education in the United States.* Boston: Houghton Mifflin Company, 1934.

Curti, Merle, *The Social Ideas of American Educators.* New York: Charles Scribner's Sons, 1935.

———, *The Growth of American Thought.* New York: Harper & Row, Publishers, Inc., 1943.

Dauer, Victor P., "The Amateur Code in American College Athletics." Ph.D. dissertation, The University of Michigan, 1949.

Davis, E. C., *Philosophic Process in Physical Education.* Philadelphia: Lea & Febiger, 1961.

———, ed. *Philosophies Fashion Physical Education.* Dubuque, Iowa: William C. Brown Company, 1963.

Dewey, John, *Democracy and Education.* New York: The Macmillan Company, 1916.

Dewhurst, F. F. *et al., America's Needs and Resources.* New York: The Twentieth Century Fund, Inc., 1947.

Diem, Carl, *Weltgeschichte des Sports und der Leibeserziehung.* Stuttgart, West Germany: J. G. Cotta'sche Buchhandlung, 1960.

Doell, C. E., and G. B. Fitzgerald, *A Brief History of Parks and Recreation.* Chicago: The Athletic Institute, 1954.

Dorgan, Ethel J., "Luther Halsey Gulick." Ph.D. dissertation, Columbia University, 1934.

Douglass, P. F. *et al.,* eds. *Recreation in the Age of Automation.* Philadelphia: *The Annals of the American Academy of Political and Social Science,* Vol. 312 (September, 1957).

Downey, Robert J., "An Identification of the Philosophical Beliefs of Educators in the Field of Health Education." Ph.D. dissertation, University of Southern California, 1956.

Drew, A. Gwendolyn, "A Historical Study of the Concern of the Federal Government for the Physical Fitness of Non-Age Youth with Reference to the Schools." Ph.D. dissertation, University of Pittsburgh, 1944.

Dulles, Foster R., *A History of Recreation* (2nd ed.). New York: Appleton-Century-Crofts Co., Inc., 1965.

Dunbar, Henry F., Jr., "A Brief History of the College Physical Education Association." Ph.D. dissertation, Columbia University, 1950.

Duncan, Isadora, *Art of the Dance.* New York: J. J. Little and Ives Co., 1928.

Durant, Will, *The Story of Philosophy* (Rev. ed.). New York: Garden City Publishing Co., Inc., 1938.

———, *Our Oriental Heritage.* New York: Simon and Schuster, 1954.

———, *The Life of Greece.* New York: Simon and Schuster, 1939.

———, *Caesar and Christ.* New York: Simon and Schuster, 1944.

———, *The Age of Faith.* New York: Simon and Schuster, 1950.

Durant, Will, *The Renaissance.* New York: Simon and Schuster, 1953.
———, *The Reformation.* New York: Simon and Schuster, 1957.
Durant, Will and Ariel, *The Age of Reason Begins.* New York: Simon and Schuster, 1961.
———, *The Age of Louis XIV.* New York: Simon and Schuster, 1963.
———, *The Age of Voltaire.* New York: Simon and Schuster, 1965.
Eby, F. and C. F. Arrowood, *The Development of Modern Education.* Englewood Cliffs, N.J.: Prentice-Hall, Inc., 1934.
———, *The History and Philosophy of Education.* Englewood Cliffs, N.J.: Prentice-Hall, Inc., 1940.
Educational Policies Commission, *Moral and Spiritual Values in the Public Schools.* Washington, D.C.: National Education Association, 1951.
———, "The Central Purpose of American Education." (Pamphlet). Washington, D.C.: National Education Association, 1961.
Ekirch, A. A., *The Idea of Progress in America.* New York: Columbia University Press, 1944.
Ellfeldt, Lois E., and Eleanor Metheny, "Movement and Meaning: Development of a General Theory," *Research Quarterly,* 29 (October, 1958), 264–73.
Ellis, Havelock, *The Dance of Life.* New York: Modern Library, 1929.
Engels, Karl, "Why Do We Dance?" *Musical Quarterly,* VI (October, 1920), 510–31.
Esslinger, Arthur A., "A Philosophical Study of Principles for Selecting Activities in Physical Education." Ph.D. dissertation, State University of Iowa, 1938.
Evans, A., *The Palace of Minos at Knossos.* London: The Macmillan Company, Five volumes, 1921–1936.
Eyler, Marvin H., "Origins of Some Modern Sports." Ph.D. dissertation, University of Illinois, 1956.
Faguet, Émile, *Initiation into Philosophy.* New York: G. P. Putnam's Sons, 1914.
Feibleman, James, *The Revival of Realism.* Chapel Hill, N.C.: The University of North Carolina Press, 1946.
"Fellowship of Christian Athletes, The." (Pamphlet). Kansas City, Missouri: Distributed by The Fellowship of Christian Athletes, January 19, 1962.
Flath, A. W., *A History of Relations between the National Collegiate Athletic Association and the Amateur Athletic Union of the United States (1905–1963).* Champaign, Ill.: Stipes Publishing Company, 1964. (Includes a Foreword by Earle F. Zeigler entitled "Amateurism, Semiprofessionalism, and Professionalism in Sport—A Persistent Educational Problem").
Frankena, William K., *Ethics.* Englewood Cliffs, N.J.: Prentice-Hall, Inc., 1963.
———, *Philosophy of Education.* New York: The Macmillan Company, 1965.
———, *Three Historical Philosophies of Education.* Chicago: Scott, Foresman and Company, 1965.
Frederick, Mary M., "Naturalism: The Philosophy of Jean Jacques Rousseau and Its Implications for American Physical Education." D.P.E. dissertation, Springfield College, 1961.
Freeman, Kenneth J., *Schools of Hellas.* London: Macmillan and Company, 1922.
Geiger, George R., "An Experimentalist Approach to Education," in *Modern Philosophies and Education,* ed. by N. B. Henry. Chicago: The University of Chicago Press, 1955.
Grasberger, L., *Erziehung und Unterricht im Klassischen Altertum.* Würzburg, Germany: Stahel'schen Buch- und Kunsthandlung, Three volumes, 1864–1881.
Graves, F. P., *A History of Education Before the Middle Ages.* New York: The Macmillan Company, 1909.

Graves, F. P., *A History of Education During the Middle Ages.* New York: The Macmillan Company, 1910.

———, *A History of Education in Modern Times.* New York: The Macmillan Company, 1913.

Greene, Theodore M., "A Liberal Christian Idealist Philosophy of Education," in *Fifty-fourth Yearbook* of the National Society for the Study of Education (Part I). Chicago, Illinois: The University of Chicago Press, 1955.

Gross, Bertram M., *The Managing of Organizations.* 2 vols. New York: Crowell-Collier Publishing Co., 1964.

Hackensmith, C. W., *History of Physical Education.* New York: Harper & Row, Publishers, 1966.

Hambly, W. D., *Tribal Dancing and Social Development.* London: Witherby, 1926.

———, and C. Hose, *Origins of Education among Primitive Peoples.* London: The Macmillan Company, 1926.

Hammond's World Atlas. New York: C. S. Hammond & Company, 1954.

Harris, H. A., *Greek Athletes and Athletics.* London: Hutchinson & Co., 1964.

Hartwell, E. M., *Physical Training.* Washington: Government Printing Office, 1899.

Hawkes, Jacquetta, and Leonard Woolley, *History of Mankind* (Vol. I, *Prehistory and the Beginnings of Civilization*). New York: Harper & Row, Publishers, 1963.

Hayes, Carlton J., *Nationalism: A Religion.* New York: The Macmillan Company, 1961.

H'Doubler, Margaret, *The Dance and Its Place in Education.* New York: Harcourt, Brace, and World, 1925.

———, *Dance, a Creative Art Experience.* New York: F. S. Crofts and Co., 1940.

Hess, Ford A., "American Objectives of Physical Education from 1900–1957 Assessed in the Light of Certain Historical Events." Ed.D. dissertation, New York University, 1959.

Hirth, F., *The Ancient History of China.* New York: Columbia University Press, 1911.

Hoover, Francis L., "A History of the National Association of Intercollegiate Athletics." P.E.D. dissertation, Indiana University, 1958.

Horne, Herman H., "An Idealistic Philosophy of Education," in *Forty-First Yearbook* of the National Society for the Study of Education (Part I). Chicago, Ill.: The University of Chicago Press, 1942.

Hospers, John, *An Introduction to Philosophical Analysis.* Englewood Cliffs, N.J.: Prentice-Hall, Inc., 1953.

Huizinga, J., *Homo Ludens: A Study of the Play-Element in Culture.* Boston: The Beacon Press, 1950.

Huxley, Julian, *New Bottles for New Wine.* New York: Harper and Row, Publishers, 1957.

Johnson, Elmer L., "A History of Physical Education in the Young Men's Christian Association." Ed.D. dissertation, University of Southern California, 1954.

Kahler, Erich, *The Meaning of History.* New York: George Braziller, Inc., 1964.

Kaplan, Abraham, *The New World of Philosophy.* New York: Random House, 1961.

Kaplan, M., *Leisure in America: A Social Inquiry.* New York: John Wiley & Sons, Inc., 1960.

Karsten, R., *The Civilization of the South American Indians.* New York: Alfred A. Knopf, Inc., 1926.

Keating, James W., "Sportsmanship as a Moral Category," *Ethics,* LXXV, No. 1 (October, 1964), 25–35.

Kees, H., *Der Opfertanz des Ägyptischen Königs.* Leipzig: J. C. Hinrichs'sche Buchhandlung, 1912.

Kidess, Atallah A., "A Study of the Work and Contributions of Dr. James Huff McCurdy to Physical Education." D.P.E. dissertation, Springfield College, 1958.

Kneller, George F., *Existentialism and Education.* New York: Philosophical Library, Inc., 1958.

Kraemer, C. J., "A Greek Element in Egyptian Dancing," *American Journal of Archaeology,* XXXV (1931), 125–38.

Lampkin, Lucy, "Dance in Art," *Research Quarterly,* 7 (May, 1936), 138.

Langer, Susanne K., *Philosophy in a New Key.* New York: The New American Library, 1948.

Langer, William L., ed. *An Encyclopedia of World History* (Rev. ed.). Boston: Houghton Mifflin Company, 1952.

Larkin, Richard A., "The Influence of John Dewey on Physical Education." M.A. thesis, The Ohio State University, 1936.

Larrabee, E., and R. Meyersohn, *Mass Leisure.* New York: The Macmillan Co., 1958.

Laurie, S., *History of Educational Opinion since the Renaissance.* New York: David McKay Co., Inc., 1900.

Lawton, W. C., *Introduction to Classical Latin Literature.* New York: Charles Scribner's Sons, 1904.

Leonard, F. E., *Pioneers of Modern Physical Training* (2nd ed.). New York: Association Press, 1915.

———, and G. B. Affleck, *The History of Physical Education* (3rd ed.). Philadelphia: Lea & Febiger, 1947.

Lexová, I., *Ancient Egyptian Dances.* Translated by K. Haltmar. Praha: Oriental Institute, 1935.

Limbert, Paul, "Physical Education, Sport, and Recreation," *World Communiqué* (January–February, 1961), 3.

Locke, Margaret C., "A Biographical Study of Agnes Rebecca Wayman: Her Life and Contributions to the Field of Health, Physical Education, and Recreation." D.P.E. dissertation, Springfield College, 1959.

Lowie, Robert H., *Primitive Religion.* New York: Boni and Liveright, 1924.

Lozes, Jewell H., "The Philosophy of Certain Religion Denominations Relative to Physical Education, and the Effect of this Philosophy on Physical Education in Certain Church-Related Institutions." M.S. thesis, Pennsylvania State University, 1955.

Lynn, Minnie L., "Major Emphases of Physical Education in the United States." Ph.D. dissertation, University of Pittsburgh, 1944.

Marique, P., *History of Christian Education.* Vols. I–III. New York: Fordham University Press, 1924–1932.

Marquardt, J., *Das Privatleben der Römer.* Leipzig: Lirzel Buchhandlung, 1886.

Marrou, H. I., *A History of Education in Antiquity.* Translated by George Lamb. New York: The New American Library of World Literature, Inc., 1964.

Martin, John, *The Dance.* New York: Tudor Publishing Co., 1946.

McCloy, C. H., *Philosophical Bases for Physical Education.* New York: Appleton-Century-Crofts, Inc., 1940.

McGucken, William J., "The Philosophy of Catholic Education," in *Forty-First Yearbook* of the National Society for the Study of Education (Part I). Chicago: The University of Chicago Press, 1942.

McIntosh, P. C., *et al. History of Physical Education.* London: Routledge & Kegan Paul, 1957.

McNeill, W. H., *The Rise of the West*. Chicago: The University of Chicago Press, 1963.

Means, R. K., *A History of Health Education in the United States*, Philadelphia: Lea & Febiger, 1962.

Metheny, Eleanor, *Connotations of Movement in Sport and Dance*. Dubuque, Iowa: Wm. C. Brown Company, Publishers, 1965.

Metzner, Henry, *A Brief History of the American Turnerbund* (Rev. ed.). Pittsburgh, Pa.: National Executive Committee of the American Turnerbund, 1924.

Meyer, A. E., *The Development of Education in the Twentieth Century*. Englewood Cliffs, N.J.: Prentice-Hall, Inc., 1939.

Meyerhoff, H., ed. *The Philosophy of History in Our Time*. New York: Doubleday & Company, Inc., 1959.

Mitchell, Elmer D., "The Growth of Physical Education and Allied Movements in the State of Michigan." Ph.D. dissertation, The University of Michigan, 1938.

Monroe, P., *Cyclopedia of Education*. New York: The Macmillan Company, 1911–1913.

———, *Source Book of the History of Education*. New York: The Macmillan Company, 1921.

Montgomery, James A., "The Growth of the Interscholastic Athletics Movement in the United States, 1890–1940." Ed.D. dissertation, George Peabody College for Teachers, 1960.

Moore, A. C., Jr., "Origins of Thirty-Three Sports." Ph.D. dissertation, University of Illinois, 1961.

Morison, Samuel Eliot, *The Oxford History of the American People*. New York: Oxford University Press, 1965.

Morland, Richard B., "A Philosophical Interpretation of the Educational Views Held by Leaders in American Physical Education." Ph.D. dissertation, New York University, 1958.

Morris, Richard B., ed. *Encyclopedia of American History* (Rev. ed.). New York: Harper & Row, Publishers, 1965.

Morris, Van Cleve, *Philosophy and the American School*. Boston: Houghton Mifflin Company, 1961.

———, *Existentialism in Education*. New York: Harper & Row, Publishers, 1966.

Mosso, A., *The Palaces of Crete and Their Builders*. London: Unwin, 1907.

Mulhern, J., *A History of Education*. New York: The Ronald Press Company, 1946.

Müller, F. M., ed. *The Sacred Books of the East*. 50 vols. Oxford: Clarendon Press, 1879–1910.

Muller, Herbert J., *The Uses of the Past*. New York: The New American Library of World Literature, Inc., 1954. (First published, London: Oxford University Press, Inc., 1952.)

———, *Freedom in the Ancient World*. New York: Harper & Row, 1961.

———, *Freedom in the Western World*. New York: Harper & Row, 1963.

———, *Religion and Freedom in the Modern World*. Chicago: The University of Chicago Press, 1963.

———, *Freedom in the Modern World*. New York: Harper & Row, 1966.

Nash, J. B., *Philosophy of Recreation and Leisure*. Dubuque, Iowa: Wm. C. Brown Company, Publishers, 1960. (First published, St. Louis: the C. V. Mosby Company, 1953)

Nash, Willard L., "A Study of the Stated Aims and Purposes of the Departments of Military Science and Tactics, and Physical Education in the Land-Grant Colleges of the United States." Ph.D. dissertation, Columbia University, 1934.

National Education Association and American Association of School Administrators, Educational Policies Commission, *School Athletics, Problems and Policies.* Washington, D.C.: The Commission, 1954.

Neumeyer, M. H., and E. S. Neumeyer, *Leisure and Recreation* (Rev. ed.). New York: The Ronald Press Company, 1958.

Nevins, Allan, *The Gateway to History.* Garden City, N.Y.: Doubleday & Company, Inc., 1962.

Oberteuffer, D., and C. Ulrich, *Physical Education* (3rd ed.). New York: Harper & Row, Publishers, 1962.

Oesterley, W. O. E., *The Sacred Dance.* New York: The Macmillan Co., 1923.

Page, Barbara, "The Philosophy of the Dance," *Research Quarterly,* IV, No. 2 (May, 1933), 5–49.

Paplauskas-Ramunas, Antoine, *L'Éducation Physique dans L'Humanisme intégral.* Ottawa, Canada: Les Éditions de l'Université d'Ottawa, 1960.

Pareti, Luigi (assisted by Paolo Brezzi and Luciano Petech), *History of Mankind* (Vol. II, *The Ancient World*). New York: Harper & Row, Publishers, 1965.

Phillips, Madge M., "Biographies of Selected Women Leaders in Physical Education in the United States." Ph.D. dissertation, State University of Iowa, 1960.

Pierro, Armstead A., "A History of Professional Preparation for Physical Education in Selected Negro Colleges and Universities, 1924–1958." Ph.D. dissertation, The University of Michigan, 1962.

Pope Pius XXI, "Physical Culture and Youth," *Catholic Newsletter,* No. 288 (May 26, 1945).

———, "Sports and Gymnastics," *Catholic Mind,* No. 51 (September, 1953), 569–76.

———, "Christian Conduct Towards Athletics," *Catholic Mind,* No. 54 (July, 1956), 409–17.

Radir, Ruth A., *Modern Dance for the Youth of America.* New York: A. S. Barnes & Co., 1944.

Rajagopalan, K., *A Brief History of Physical Education in India.* Delhi: Army Publishers, 1963.

Ray, Harold L., "The Life and Professional Contribution of William Gilbert Anderson, M.D." Ph.D. dissertation, Ohio State University, 1959.

Reisner, E. H., *Nationalism and Education since 1789.* New York: The Macmillan Company, 1925.

———, *Historical Foundations of Modern Education.* New York: The Macmillan Company, 1927.

Rice, E. A., J. L. Hutchinson, and Mabel Lee, *A Brief History of Physical Education* (4th ed.). New York: The Ronald Press Company, 1958.

Robinson, Rachel S., *Sources for the History of Greek Athletics* (Rev. ed.). Cincinnati, Ohio: Published by the Author, 338 Probasco St., 1955.

Sachs, Curt, *World History of the Dance.* New York: W. W. Norton & Company, Inc., 1937.

Sapora, A. V., and E. D. Mitchell, *The Theory of Play and Recreation* (3rd ed.). New York: The Ronald Press Company, 1961.

Savage, H. J., *et al., American College Athletics.* New York: The Carnegie Foundation for the Advancement of Teaching, 1929.

Schutte, Fred, "Objectives of Physical Education in the United States, 1870–1929." M.A. thesis, New York University, 1930.

Schwendener, N., *A History of Physical Education in the United States.* New York: A. S. Barnes & Co., 1942.

Scott, H. A., *Competitive Sports in Schools and Colleges.* New York: Harper & Row, Publishers, Inc., 1951.

Setton, Kenneth M., "A New Look at Medieval Europe," *National Geographic*, Vol. 122, No. 6 (December, 1962), 798–859.

Sharp, Cecil, and O. P. Oppe, *An Historical Survey of Dancing in Europe*. New York: Minton Balch and Company, 1924.

Shepard, Natalie M., "Democracy in Physical Education: A Study of the Implications for Educating for Democracy through Physical Education." Ed.D. dissertation, New York University, 1952.

Shivers, Jay S., "An Analysis of Theories of Recreation." Ph.D. dissertation, University of Wisconsin, 1958.

Sigerist, Henry E., *Landmarks in the History of Hygiene*. London: Oxford University Press, 1956.

Simpson, George G., *The Meaning of Evolution*. New Haven and London: Yale University Press, 1949.

Slatton, Yvonne L., "The Philosophical Beliefs of Undergraduates and Graduate Physical Education Major Students and the Physical Education Faculty at the University of North Carolina at Greensboro." M.S. thesis, University of North Carolina at Greensboro, 1964.

Slusher, Howard S., "Existentialism and Physical Education." A paper presented to the American Association for Health, Physical Education, and Recreation Convention (History and Philosophy Section), May 3, 1963. (An abridged version appeared in *The Physical Educator*, Vol. 20, No. 4 (December, 1963), 153–56.

Smith, Glenn M., "The History of the Society of State Directors of Health and Physical Education." Ph.D. dissertation, Columbia University, 1953.

Snyder, R. A., and H. A. Scott, *Professional Preparation in Health, Physical Education, and Recreation*. New York: McGraw-Hill Book Company, Inc., 1954.

Spears, Betty M., "Philosophical Bases for Physical Education Experiences Consistent with the Goals of General Education for College Women." Ph.D. dissertation, New York University, 1956.

Spencer, Herbert, *Education: Intellectual, Moral, and Physical*. London: Watts & Co., 1949.

Stagg, Paul, "The Development of the National Collegiate Athletic Association in Relationship to Intercollegiate Athletics in the United States." Ph.D. dissertation, New York University, 1947.

Toynbee, Arnold J. (Abridgement of Vols. I–VI by D. C. Somervell), *A Study of History*. New York and London: Oxford University Press, 1947.

Trekell, Marianna, "Gertrude Evelyn Moulton, M.D.; Her Life and Professional Career in Health and Physical Education." Ph.D. dissertation, Ohio State University, 1963.

Ulich, R., *History of Educational Thought*. New York: America Book Co., 1945.

Ulrich, Celeste, "Historical Bibliography, Part I," *JOHPER*, Vol. 31, No. 4 (April, 1960), 100–1.

———, "Historical Bibliography, Part II," *JOHPER*, Vol. 31, No. 5 (May–June, 1960), 45–6.

Van Dalen, D. B., E. D. Mitchell, and B. L. Bennett, *A World History of Physical Education*. Englewood Cliffs, N.J.: Prentice-Hall, Inc., 1953.

VanderZwaag, Harold J., "Nationalism in American Physical Education," in *Proceedings* of the National College Physical Education Association for Men (December 27–29, 1965), 35–40.

Van Loon, H. W., *The Arts*. New York: Simon and Schuster, 1937.

Van Vliet, M. L., ed., *Physical Education in Canada*. Scarborough, Ontario: Prentice-Hall of Canada, Ltd., 1965.

Vuillier, Gaston, *History of Dancing*. New York: Appleton-Century-Crofts, 1897.

Washke, Paul R., "The Development of the American Association for Health, Physical Education, and Recreation and its Relationship to Physical Education in the United States." Ph.D. dissertation, New York University, 1943.

Watts, Doris P., "Changing Conceptions of Competitive Sports for Girls and Women in the United States from 1880 to 1960." Ph.D. dissertation, University of California at Los Angeles, 1960.

Weaver, R. B., *Amusement and Sports in American Life.* Chicago: The University of Chicago Press, 1939.

Webster, Randolph, *Philosophy of Physical Education.* Dubuque, Iowa: Wm. C. Brown Company, Publishers, 1965.

Weir, L. H., *Europe at Play.* New York: A. S. Barnes & Co., 1937.

Welch, J. E., "Edward Hitchcock, M.D., Founder of Physical Education in the College Curriculum." Ed.D. dissertation, George Peabody College for Teachers, 1962.

Weston, A., *The Making of American Physical Education.* New York: Appleton-Century-Crofts, Inc., 1962.

Whitehead, Alfred N., *The Aims of Education.* New York: The Macmillan Company, 1929.

Wild, John, "Education and Human Society: A Realistic View," in the *Fifty-Fourth Yearbook* of the National Society for the Study of Education (Part I). Chicago: The University of Chicago Press, 1955.

Wilds, E. H., *Foundations of Modern Education.* New York: Holt, Rinehart & Winston, Inc., 1942.

Wilkinson, J. G., *The Manners and Customs of the Ancient Egyptians.* 3 vols. Boston: Cassino, 1883.

Williams, Jane E., *Ancient Art and Ritual.* London: Oxford University Press, 1943.

Williams, Jesse F., *The Principles of Physical Education* (8th ed.). Philadelphia: W. B. Saunders Co., 1964.

Williams, J. Paul, *What Americans Believe and How They Worship.* New York: Harper & Row, Publishers, 1952.

Wilton, Wilton M., "A Comparative Analysis of Theories Related to Moral and Spiritual Values in Physical Education." Ed.D. dissertation, University of California at Los Angeles, 1956.

Wood, Thomas D., and Rosalind F. Cassidy, *The New Physical Education.* New York: The Macmillan Company, 1927.

Woodward, W. H., *Vittorino da Feltre and Other Humanist Educators.* Cambridge: Cambridge University Press, 1905.

Woody, Thomas, *Life and Education in Early Societies.* New York: The Macmillan Company, 1949.

Y.M.C.A., *A New Yook at YMCA Physical Education.* New York: Association Press, 1959.

Zeigler, Earle F., "A History of Professional Preparation for Physical Education in the United States, 1861–1948." Ph.D. dissertation, Yale University, 1951. (Published by Microcard Publications, University of Oregon at Eugene).

————, *Administration of Physical Education and Athletics: The Case Method Approach.* Englewood Cliffs, N.J.: Prentice-Hall, Inc., 1959.

————, *Philosophical Foundations for Physical, Health, and Recreation Education.* Englewood Cliffs, N.J.: Prentice-Hall, Inc., 1964.

————, *A Brief Introduction to the Philosophy of Religion.* Champaign, Ill.: Stipes Publishing Company, 1965.

————, and H. J. VanderZwaag, *Physical Education: Reconstructionism or Essentialism?* Champaign, Ill.: Stipes Publishing Company, 1966.

Index